25
Words
OR
Less

Advance Praise for *25 Words or Less*

*"If I'd known then what I know after devouring this riveting how-to,
I'd have had a swarm of suitors from which to choose my ideal mate."*

—Patricia Smith, columnist, the *Boston Globe*

*"Minsky and Calvo have taken proven marketing principles
and turned them into tactics for finding romance. Guaranteed
to fill the void in any love life."*

—Kevin Tynan, author of *Exposure! How to Market So Your
Message Is Unavoidable,* and president, Tynan Marketing

*"If your poetry doesn't get you a date, here's a book
that will. Hey, you can even make your ad a poem —
just don't make it rhyme."*

—Marc Smith, poet, founder of the
Uptown Poetry Slam

25 Words OR Less

How to Write Like a Pro to Find That
Special Someone Through Personal Ads

Emily Thornton Calvo
Laurence Minsky

CB
CONTEMPORARY BOOKS

Library of Congress Cataloging-in-Publication Data

Calvo, Emily Thornton
    25 words or less : how to write like a pro to find that special someone through personal ads / Emily Thornton Calvo and Laurence Minsky.
       p.   cm.
   ISBN 0-8092-2878-5
    1. Mate selection.   2. Dating (Social customs).   3. Single people—Social networks.   4. Personals.   5. English language—Usage.   I. Laurence Minsky.
II. Title.
PIQ801.C2728   1998
646.7'7—dc21   97-43788
                                              CIP

Cover design by Mary Lockwood
Cover image copyright © Mona Daly/Artville, LLC
Interior design by Herman Adler Design Group

Published by Contemporary Books
A division of NTC/Contemporary Publishing Group, Inc.
4255 West Touhy Avenue, Lincolnwood (Chicago), Illinois 60646-1975 U.S.A.
Copyright © 1998 by Emily Thornton Calvo and Laurence Minsky
All rights reserved. No part of this book may be reproduced, stored in a retrieval system, or transmitted in any form or by any means, electronic, mechanical, photocopying, recording, or otherwise, without the prior permission of NTC/Contemporary Publishing Group, Inc.
Printed in the United States of America
International Standard Book Number: 0-8092-2878-5

15   14   13   12   11   10   9   8   7   6   5   4   3   2   1

Also by Minsky and Calvo

How to Succeed in Advertising When All You Have Is Talent

Contents

Foreword

Does this sound familiar? You only intend to get something cold to drink at the local Quick Trip and on the way back to your car, you stop by the rusty rack outside and scan the selection of local magazines chock-full of personal ads. You can't resist picking up the copy with a picture of a good-looking couple proclaimed to be its most recent personal-ad success story. Suddenly you find yourself scanning the personals—strictly for entertainment purposes, of course. You flip over to whatever section fits you to see what kind of people are there. Oh, what fun!

You notice that the same words always seem to pop up: *attractive, fun loving, fit.* Pretty redundant, huh? The people all appear to be exercise freaks who love to have fun and love the outdoors. Surely they exaggerate. You think your chances of meeting that special someone in this motley crew are about as slim as winning the lottery.

What kind of a person would really advertise for a love partner? It would have to be someone who can't get a date—a social outcast, right? That person must be fifty pounds overweight, be totally desperate for love, or look like Elmer Fudd or Olive Oyle. Your thoughts turn to who would actually be brave enough to call the phone number listed at the end of the ad. Just how much cash would someone be willing to part with to place these silly ads or call that 900-number?

Our passion to find a companion with whom we can share laughs, have fun, or perhaps even spend the rest of our life is so strong that we often go to almost any lengths to make the connection—which makes personal ads a big business. You see them everywhere: magazines, newspapers, television, radio, and even billboards. High-tech personal ads appear on the Internet and the on-line services.

If you are willing to learn the strategies of placing an ad, how to maximize results with the right words, how to return calls, how to introduce yourself, and where to place the ad, you may be in for a great surprise. Sometimes personal ads work.

While some might scoff at the thought of advertising for a partner, there are many successful relationships that have occurred as a result of personal ads. This fact tells me that personal ads have become a viable way to attract a companion. Personal ads have come of age.

Advertising yourself is a fun way to meet people. It's about meeting people for the purpose of having someone special in your life, to have someone to talk with, to develop a healthy love relationship with, to explore mutual interests, or just to have the fun of meeting new friends. In *25 Words or Less,* Minsky and Calvo refine the art of the personals to a distinct science.

You will need to apply the appropriate safety precautions. Never give anyone your home or work address, and avoid home phone numbers until you know them better. Meet in busy public places, preferably in the afternoon. Avoid romantic dinners. When you discover someone you want to meet, ask if you may bring a friend. If your date freaks, run the other way.

Once you overcome the initial safety concerns, there are other issues to keep in mind. My work with Dr. John Gray, Ph.D., author of *Men Are from Mars, Women Are from Venus,* as host of his on-line chat room and my nationally presented Relationship Enrichment LoveShops, has highlighted two of the most common problems that occur in relationships. Being aware of these problems should help you use the personals more successfully.

The first and most common problem is undelivered communications. When meeting singles through the personals, it is wise to play your cards close until you have had several face-to-face meetings and feel comfortable enough to begin fully sharing yourself. This occurs naturally—when there is a real connection and a mutual attraction, and you both choose to pursue a relationship together.

But too often we withhold what we know really needs to be said, and by doing so, we temporarily shut down communication. Trust is the foundation of all healthy love relationships. Yet there can be no trust without conversation and no genuine intimacy without trust. One of the secrets to a healthy love relationship is never to be afraid to openly and honestly discuss whatever is relevant to its success.

The second problem is unfulfilled expectations. When looking for a serious love relationship in the personal ads, it is important to put aside your expectations about how you think things will happen. When we expect a potential partner to respond to us in a certain way and he or she doesn't, we are disappointed. Instead, focus on what you *need* from the relationship.

Everyone needs love. We can best fulfill this need by first discovering what we need as individuals, then communicating those needs. It's time to learn about doing that through the personals from the experts. So . . . get on with it. Enjoy!

Celebrate love!

Larry James
Scottsdale, Arizona

Larry James is a professional speaker and author of *Red Hot LoveNotes for Lovers, How to Really Love the One You're With,* and *LoveNotes for Lovers: Words That Make Music for Two Hearts Dancing.* He is on staff with Dr. John Gray.

Preface

Why How-To Books Don't Work and
How to Work with What Does

Ever get one of those books that tells you how to do something—the ones that give you the step-by-step rules? They take a snapshot of the idealized world and then expect you to fit in it. They don't take into account your unique background or your particular likes and dislikes—the quirky traits that make you an individual.

With books on dating, this is even more common. Many of these how-to books expect that everyone wants the same sort of relationship (marriage); see themselves as the same kind of people (*GQ* guys and *Cosmo* girls); and look for their perfect complement.

But think about it: if you fit into a mold, you probably would be pretty boring. Inevitably, following the how-to path that authors typically present can lead to frustration and feelings of inadequacy. You might even begin to ask yourself, "What's wrong with me?"

Our answer: nothing. The books are wrong.

Even Detroit, in the world of automotive commerce, has discovered that people have distinct tastes, interests, and personalities. It's the era of customization. Just look at the wider array of choices in car brands—and all of the options you can get with a new car.

It's time that the writers of self-help books on cultivating relationships get with the program.

In our previous book, *How to Succeed in Advertising When All You Have Is Talent*, we even went so far as to print conflicting advice (with the rationale behind it) and invited our readers to choose the path that best fit them. Here we don't go quite that far.

In this book, we cover creative problem-solving techniques, expand your options with the personals, help you generate ideas, and give you the background for creating an effective personal of your own. You're in charge of your destiny. The ultimate solution will come from you and your situation. You're the expert on what's right for you. Take and use the ideas that fit your needs rather than trying to make yourself fit the specific ideas in this book. Our process allows for that.

Personal ads can open up a world of opportunities. But you must choose the options that are best for you. We'll give you the techniques. The rest is up to you.

Acknowledgments

Mark Twain once wrote that "all you need in life is ignorance and confidence, and then success is sure." But that's not really all of it. You also need the encouragement, support, and advice of other people.

Our special thanks to Julie Rigby and Patty Leibenthal for their insights into today's dating scene; Cathy Luchetti for her insights into yesterday's dating scene; Laurie Hoppe for messenger services; J. J. Bittenbinder for his expertise in personal safety; Rita Steiskal of Storandt/Pann/Margolis for her media expertise; Connie Milbourne of Frankel and Company and Sue Viecelli of Thompson Specialized Communications for their insights into traditional consumer- and recruitment-advertising methods; Phil Ginnodo, Pamela Liebig, and Marlene Colella for story leads; Lynn Leinartas of Frankel and Company and the third floor research librarians at the Evanston Public Library for help in finding background material; our agents Nicholas Smith and Andrea Pedolsky at the Altair Literary Agency and Betsy Lancefield, Gerilee Hundt, and Rich Hagle of NTC/Contemporary for their enthusiasm and belief in this project; Stephanie Di Tullio of NTC/Contemporary and Liane Adduci-Urevig of Frankel and Company for their help in making the book a success; Christy Calvo and Veronica Calvo for weathering their mother's dating experiences; Rhonda Present for her patience, encouragement, and understanding of her husband's need to write while pressing chores were waiting at home; Jeanne Rumpsa for encouragement; Laura Bensman, Bill Rosen, Jim Polowy, and Lor Gold at Frankel and Company and Gary Storandt, Nick Pann, and Larry Margolis at Storandt/Pann/Margolis for their ongoing support as well as for recognizing that our minds really were focused on our jobs during our working hours; and the more than 100 people who unselfishly gave us permission to use their stories and ads (their names have been changed) and shared their hopes, dreams, and experiences with us—and you—in the pages of this book.

25
Words
OR
Less

Getting *Personal*

When you meet someone at a party, you fall in love from the outside in.
When you meet someone through the personals, you fall in love from the inside out.

—A personal-ad user

A few years ago, Maggie attended a party that was thrown by a very successful male attorney. He invited dozens of single acquaintances hoping sparks would fly. Knowing this man's friends were generally an eclectic group of intelligent and adventurous people, Maggie knew she'd have a wonderful time. And it wasn't long before a man in the corner of the room had her attention. He was just her type—longish dark hair and a neat beard. He wore a black turtleneck with a casual jacket. Sort of swarthy looking, but with an intellectual slant. He was quiet and spent some time writing in a notebook. As a writer, Maggie was intrigued.

Throughout the evening, their eyes met. A friend challenged her to approach him before the night was over—while generally outgoing, approaching men she found attractive was difficult for Maggie. About 10 minutes before she had planned to leave—knowing she'd never respect herself if she didn't say something—she stood up and inched her way across the room.

"So what are you writing about?" Maggie said, grasping at the obvious, hoping this would start a conversation. He looked up at her, his mouth hanging open. He held his stare for a long time. A very long time.

"I'm trying to write out the lyrics to all the Dead songs. You know, the Grateful Dead," he replied with pride.

"Oh," she said. Not being particularly impressed, Maggie didn't know how to respond. And not being particularly rude, she didn't walk away instantly. In the brief conversation that followed, she learned that he was the assistant of another guest at the party who had planned to drive him home. And while she felt he was the most physically attractive man in the room, his immediate personal goal of transcribing the lyrics of Grateful Dead songs was a turnoff.

Yes, you *can* meet someone at a bar, a church group, or a singles event and form a satisfying relationship—especially if attraction hinges on your partner's appearance. But Maggie's story is more typical. You hear these complaints all the time:

- "It's so difficult to meet anyone."
- "All the good ones are taken."
- "I'm too old for the bar scene."
- "The singles scene is so superficial."

Why do people make these complaints? Because singles events and the bar scene only offer a start. If other qualities are important to you, going to a bar or an event to meet someone offers limited opportunities to meet the right person for you. In fact, in our research for this book we found that the men and women who relied solely on chance encounters to find someone to date were the same individuals who whined about how difficult it is to meet quality people.

Here's why. Imagine that you're in a bar or at a singles party. All of a sudden the most stunning woman or the handsomest man captures your attention—he or she is just your type.

You may have already talked with several people who seemed interesting and nice, but this one is special. What's more, you detect a mutual attraction. Your antenna goes up. It locks on your target. You move toward each other. Strike up a conversation. Discover you like the same movies. Go to the same clubs. Go in-line skating at the same park.

You're ecstatic. "finally," you think, "this is the person I've been looking for."

Then, he or she takes out a cigarette. Or reaches for a third Long Island iced tea. Or tells you how *this time* rehab really worked. Whatever turns you off, by the end of the evening, you feel you've wasted your time.

Even more disturbing is the fact that you've missed the opportunity to connect with other people. Maybe your perfect match was the woman with the big nose and frizzy hair or the guy with the paunch. No way? What if you found out that the frizzy-haired woman is a chef in her own French restaurant? What if that guy with the paunch owns a successful ski resort? Many times, it's the hidden qualities that make a person seem more attractive. Just consider some of the people you've cared for and the qualities you found attractive in them. How would you have rated them at first sight? Or consider how you would resent being evaluated by strangers without them knowing all your wonderful qualities—beyond simply your appearance. Personal ads allow you to identify something that's attractive about a person before his or her appearance has a chance to sway your opinion.

Consider Sally's experience dating through the personals. A 29-year-old massage therapist, she's been using personals for more than three years now and reports that she's developed many strong friendships because of it. "If one moves toward marriage, cool," she says. "But I just want someone to participate in life with me and to grow with me." She turned to the personals when she received a wedding invitation that read, "What a personal ad hath put together, let no man put asunder."

Preferring to respond to the ads rather than place one, she circles the personals that appeal to her. "I get a sense of the type of person behind an ad by the style in which it's been written," she reports. "I want to be moved, to laugh, or to be inspired in some way—or to simply get the facts that are in line with my interests and beliefs."

After compiling her list, she then whittles it down to the five or six ads that best fit the qualities she's seeking and then listens to their voice-mail recordings. "If one doesn't sound authentic, then I don't leave a message," she says. When she does leave a message, she gives her name, phone number, why she enjoyed reading the ad, and the qualities she shares with the advertiser. She closes by saying, "If you're interested in continuing this conversation, call."

Almost all of her messages get a response. She usually arranges to meet at a local coffee shop or bar on a weeknight, so that she has a natural reason to end the evening. Since most of her dates have gone well (she only reports three duds), introduced her to people she never would have met, and allowed her to form three ongoing friendships, she's committed to the personals and now looks forward to placing her own ad. "It's the only way I date now," she says.

Sally recognizes that it's difficult to form a meaningful bond with someone when you don't know what's really on the inside. Sometimes the guy in the Harley jacket writes poetry. The woman with the nose ring voted Republican. Human beings are complex. Each one has layer upon layer of good and bad experiences. And each has unique personality traits, values, and habits. You never know who has the heart of gold. So when you let appearance be your driving factor, you'll find yourself traveling on a lot of dead-end streets. This, of course, doesn't mean that you can't meet someone wonderful at a party or even on a blind date. It happens all the time. This just means that personal ads can be much more effective and efficient for you, helping you avoid heartache and giving you many more opportunities to meet Mr. or Ms. Right. And believe it or not, many of the people who use the personals are some of the most physically attractive.

A Few Important Dates in History

The struggle to find a suitable mate is not a new problem. William Fielding, in his book *Strange Customs of Courtship and Marriage,* says that this is why many cultures throughout history—from the American Indians to Eastern Europeans (who still employ professional matchmakers)—consider matchmaking to be an honored profession. (And if movies like *Crossing Delancey* are any indication, matchmakers are still in use in the United States, too.) And don't forget that the dating service—video, computer, or otherwise—is the modern version of the matchmaker. We've also all heard stories of parents arranging marriages, which still goes on in many Middle Eastern countries. (Not to mention your meddlesome mother, who has good intentions but poor taste, when she tries talking you into a blind date with the grown, stay-at-home kid of her best friend's cousin.)

This struggle is also what brought about the existence of the modern personal ad during the time of America's westward expansion. According to Cathy Luchetti, author of *I Do! Courtship, Love, and Marriage on the American Frontier,* people were becoming more mobile during this period, moving from one part of the country to another. In addition, there was an imbalance of bachelors in the West and widows in the East, and the concept of romantic love was beginning to take hold in America. It was also the start of the suffragist movement, which resulted in a demand for greater independence among young women. The economic necessities of life on the frontier also forced a greater equality among the sexes. The result? Women and men had more choice in their selection of a life mate, but fewer opportunities to meet eligible partners.

Seizing on this opportunity, newspaper publishers began to carry advertisements—and start publications—designed to match women with male settlers. Ads were placed for an exorbitant price of $1.50 per word. And if a marriage would take place as a result of the ad, an additional fee was charged to the couple. The name of the advertiser, of course, was withheld.

Some of the ads, excluding the word choices, sound as if they could have been run today. For instance, here's a sampling from 1873. They come from *The Matrimonial News,* a San Francisco newspaper that ran personal ads of "worthy" marriage prospects.

A bachelor of 40, good appearance and substantial means wants a wife. She must be under 30, amiable and musical.

A lady, 23, fair, and good looking, without means, would like to hear from a gentleman of position wanting a wife. She is well educated, accomplished, amiable and affectionate.

"Candid" seeks to improve his condition by marriage. Aged 27, height 5 feet 9 inches, dark hair and eyes, considered by all handsome, his friends unite in saying he is amiable and will make a model husband. He has not resided in California long. The lady must be one of the most extended acceptation of the word since the advertiser moves in the most polished and refined society. It is also desirable that she should have considerable money.

Another newspaper, the *Water-Cure Journal,* ran this ad in 1856:

I seek a congenial spirit if she is of the EARNEST, BRAVE, and TRUE, well-developed brain and body, a warm and willing hand. . . Am 23, medium height, size of brain 23 inches, temperament, nervous-anguine [sic]: . . . anti-rum, slavery, drug, tea, and coffe [sic] and am a vegetarian. . . shall be happy to communicate with anyone interested.

How did the personal-ad romances of the Old West turn out? Well, just like today, there were good experiences—and bad. *The Devil's Lake Journal,* a North Dakota newspaper, reported in its May 8, 1912, edition on the story of John Bartley, a prosperous farmer who placed an ad that caught the attention of a grandmother from Minnesota. The woman's granddaughter corresponded with the farmer for a year before traveling to meet him at a train depot. They married not long after that.

The *Wahpeton Times,* another newspaper in North Dakota, on March 9, 1911, reported the story of two young women who traveled there from a town in New York to meet a farmer who had been corresponding with one of the women after she'd responded to his ad. Her friend came along; because she had been so excited about the prospect of her friend's marriage, she thought she might find a husband as well. But upon seeing the farmer, the bride-to-be decided that he wasn't for her and both women returned home.

Back in the 1800s, newspapers did offer some protection to the respondents; if an advertiser was later proven to be dishonest, had questionable intentions, or was what they called a scoundrel and word got back, the newspaper would punish that person by printing his or her name.

While personal ads continued to be used throughout the years, their current rise in popularity corresponded with the rise of the counterculture and the women's movement in the 1960s and 1970s. Again there was a greater freedom to experiment and choose but few opportunities for like-minded people to meet. And there was a greater opportunity to place a personal ad. To cater to the counterculture, weekly alternative newspapers were launched all over the country. They were more open-minded than the general media. The personals in them gave people who didn't fit into the mainstream a chance to meet.

During their rise in popularity, the personals were also used by people whose special interests or locations made meeting new people difficult (they ranged—then as now—from farmers to single parents to S & M enthusiasts). For instance, there was *Sweetheart,* a magazine filled with personal ads for people living in the isolated parts of Montana, Wyoming, and North and South Dakota; this magazine became so popular that *People* magazine did a story on its founder and publisher in 1993, reporting that it had achieved a readership of more than 15,000. And in the 1980s, there was *Alaskan Man,* a magazine filled with personal ads from hearty men looking for women from the continental United States.

Since the late 1970s, the use of personal ads has gained such wide acceptance that only four major U.S. daily newspapers currently do not run them: *USA Today;* the *Dallas Morning News;* the *New York Times;* and the *Wall Street Journal.* All of the other major daily newspapers in America, approximately 1,700 publications in all, feature personal ads at least once a week. And they're even more popular in weekly papers. There are also dozens of special-interest publications dedicated solely to publishing personals throughout the country. Of course, on the international scene, there are dozens of tabloids filled with ads seeking to match foreign women with American men. You can also find personal ads more and more in magazines, on radio and cable television, and, of course, on-line.

No longer a desperate act of a lonely heart, they're now used by the general population, covering all demographic levels and political affiliations. And they can no longer be relegated to the world of the steamy and the seedy.

Needless to say, personal ads have become big business. According to an article in *U.S. News and World Report,* magazine and newspaper personals generate more than $500 million in revenues a year (dating services in the United States have annual revenues of $1 billion). A representative from one of the three companies that manages the 900-number response lines for all of the newspaper personals in the United States told us that his organization receives more than a million calls a day. (And this does not include mail, e-mail, and other ways of responding to the personals.) Industry publications report that the personals section of the classifieds is one of the most profitable areas in a newspaper—and it's virtually recession-proof!

Why are personal ads so popular? Because people are simply busier and more mobile. And because we as a culture have become more isolated. Faith Popcorn, who first identified the phenomenon of "cocooning"—a retreat into the controllable confines of one's own home to protect oneself from our increasingly stressful and violent society—now says in her book *Clicking* that this trend has become even more fortified. Why? Because people are afraid—and home is one of the few places we can feel protected. But by putting walls up around ourselves, it of course becomes harder to meet new people.

In addition, the growth in the use of personal ads is also due to a simple numbers game. Simply stated, there are now more single adults in America. In fact, the February 10, 1997, issue of *U.S. News and World Report* states that the number of people living alone has grown from 28 percent of the population in 1970 to 39 percent today. And we can only see this trend continuing.

The result? Personal ads genuinely fill a need in our lives, giving us a faster, more efficient avenue to connect with others. In fact, they're fun, they're easy, they're empowering, they're inexpensive, and they can break through the cocoon, exposing you to tons of dates in a matter of days—if not hours. Talk about instant gratification in the world of romance! Could a church picnic or your favorite bar ever do this for you?

Working at Love

Undeniably, looking for a partner today is similar to job hunting. In both cases, you are searching for a mutually satisfying relationship. And whether you want to moonlight or to commit to climbing the corporate ladder, reaching your goal takes work.

When you're seeking a new job, you spend time at it. You organize and take a systematic approach. You write a résumé and a cover letter to advertise your skills and accomplishments. You send them to companies that are advertising positions that match your background and your interests. You go on interviews that may be scary, intimidating, or disappointing. You get rejected; and if you're unemployed, your self-esteem almost always declines. Yet, even if a job seeker feels hopeless about going on yet another interview, he or she must keep answering ads, scheduling interviews, and of course, following up to land the job—much like the effort required to meet your perfect match.

Just like those unemployed people who wind up watching hours of daytime TV, it's easy for a sensitive person frustrated by relationships to slip into a rut of solitary dinners and cat grooming. As with a job search, answering or placing ads should not be your only strategy—or one that is ignored. Even though many people meet other people through networking, at bars or events, or just through sheer luck, personal ads increase your odds of finding the right match.

Unlike searching for a job, personal ads also enable you to take control and place an ad. Then your role becomes more like that of an employer.

When you're looking for a person to date, you are doing the same thing a company does when looking for an employee. Your recruitment ad must sell yourself—just like a want ad must sell a company. And you also want to find the right match. Two jobs at two different companies can have the same title but be completely different. It's the job of the want ad not only to catch the reader's attention, but to filter out potential candidates who are not a good fit. After all, landing a position that's not a good fit doesn't do anyone any good. This is the same role that you want your personal ad to play. The better you target your ad, the better your chances of finding someone who is right for you.

Researchers study how people present themselves as products and advertisers use this to their advantage when communicating to you in media advertising. So why shouldn't you use this same concept to your advantage?

While none of this may sound as romantic as you'd like, there's a magical connection that needs to be made when searching for a job—just like there's a magical connection you need to make when seeking a romance. Personal ads can be a great way to put you in the game for making that connection.

Make a Date to Experiment

If you're skeptical about placing an ad, just try it. That's what Cindi did. Fresh out of a 14-year marriage, Cindi, along with a few of her girlfriends, wondered why they were sitting around watching movies on Saturday nights. It didn't take too many Saturday nights before they decided to explore the personals and see what could, would, or might happen. Not seriously, of course. Just for fun. Just to break the monotony of renting movies.

To enhance the entertainment value of their endeavor, they decided to write ads for each other. They placed the ads in one of the more unconventional newspapers—to ensure even greater entertainment value.

Because the publication they chose had not yet installed voice mail, they had to wait about a week for the responses to begin rolling in. Each of the three women received about 15 letters. One was from an actor/model who enclosed an 8″ x 10″. Another was a form letter from a musician with an invitation to attend his next gig. One enclosed a Polaroid close-up of his penis. But many letters came from all types of guys who were just interested in meeting someone nice. Considering the lack of integrity with which the ad was placed, the interest was a pleasant surprise.

"What would happen," Cindi wondered, "if I put a little effort into writing an ad to actually attract the right guy?" Though she didn't expect to respond to any letters, Cindi placed another ad. This time she received about 25 letters. She was overwhelmed. She talked to a few of the men on the phone, but since she hadn't expected to spend time following up, work and family pressures kept her from taking the time to get to know them. Time slipped away and she was too embarrassed to call. A few more years flew by as Cindi dated dozens of men she met at parties, through friends, or at singles events.

"What would happen," Cindi then wondered, "if I wrote an ad designed to attract the man of my dreams and I committed time to actually meeting the respondents?"

She again placed an ad. This time she received fewer letters, but the men were closer to the type she was seeking. She met four of them. Although none were the love of her life, she formed longtime friendships with two of them.

Cindi's experience shows that placing a personal ad doesn't have to be a desperate, last-ditch effort to meet the partner of your dreams. It's just another way to meet people for dates who have the same interests as yours. So what do you have to lose? Try the personals. Have fun with it. And see what happens.

Why You'll Love the Personals

If our stories didn't convince you that dating through the personals is an acceptable way to meet people, then consider the following points. They sum up many of the benefits you will find.

Reach More People More Quickly

The major advantage to using personal ads is that you can very quickly meet many people who are compatible. Millions of people are placing and responding to personal ads each year, so your pool of potential partners is significant.

In the Chicago area alone, the third-largest market in the nation, we found 12 newspapers and magazines with a collective readership of 4.3 million running personal ads. Combined, they published about 1,680,000 personal ads annually. Smaller areas have proportionately similar numbers of personal ads. Even in a small town in Wisconsin, the *Eau Claire Leader Telegram* runs an average of over 100 ads a week.

These numbers only represent people who place ads, not the millions of people who respond to them. In the emerging area of radio personals, one service handles approximately 35,000 calls per month. What's more, according to a March 1997 article in the newspaper industry's trade publication *Editor and Publisher,* the average advertiser receives 10 to 15 responses each week to a personal ad (our research indicates that it's closer to 7)—and some receive as many as 100. How many nights out would it take you to contact and screen 100 people? With personal ads, you can condense years of searching into months or even days.

And how do personal ads compare to dating services? Well, consider the comments of Jeff. "I'd never go to a dating service," he said. "They're for people who are afraid. If I place a classified ad, it can go out to more than 80,000 people in one shot and I can get 16 people to date for the five dollars it cost to place the ad. But dating services are limited by the people who sign up—and cost hundreds more."

Control the Quality of the People You Meet

Looking for a successful, upscale partner? A trendy, artsy person? Personal ads allow you to target your audience. While our research tells us that the number of people using personal ads represents a cross section of society, the audience you actually reach depends on the publication in which your ad appears. An upscale magazine will generate responses from an upscale audience. A weekly alternative newspaper will expose your ad to a younger, more liberal crowd.

Meet Compatible People

What's most important to you in a partner? A desire to raise a family? The same religious background? Honesty? Or just having someone to share your season tickets to the Knicks? Personal ads allow you to specify the qualities that are important to you. There's no need to be shy about requesting responses from people with specific characteristics. This is your opportunity to target the people who most interest you. And even if you don't find the perfect partner, you're more likely to gain a friend when you've based your ad on sharing common interests.

Maintain Your Privacy

Personal ads are ideal for people who want to keep their private lives private. Your friends, family, and coworkers don't have to know you're dating. You don't have to worry about friendships lost over blind dates that don't work out. Privacy is especially valuable if you have a high-profile career. It's also important to people looking for a partner, straight or gay, who have uncommon sexual interests.

Making the Personals Work

You're probably feeling skeptical, wondering if an ad can really help you meet someone wonderful. And we're not going to promise you that it will. But we will *show you* that personal ads *do work* for many people. And you can be one of them.

In the following chapters we'll also show you how to maximize your results. After all, as we've already said, the personals are a big business. So shouldn't you get the biggest return for the time and money you invest? (Many of the ideas expressed in this book can also work for you if you use a dating service, which is even bigger business and requires a much bigger financial investment on your part. If you plan to use a dating service, work through Chapters 2 through 4 and supply the information to the dating service staff—even if they don't ask for it—because it will help them better target their search for you.)

In preparing to write this book, we interviewed more than 100 people who have dated through the personals. In the following pages, you'll find many of the secrets of their success, combined with our marketing expertise. You should note, however, that we did not interview people who were looking for ways to cheat on existing partners (that's a book for someone else to write), so if that's on your agenda, we probably can't help you (and neither can many of the more established newspapers like the *Chicago Tribune,* which don't take ads from married people). You should also note that dating through the personals can change your life. So before you begin, here are some things to remember.

Keep an Open Mind

The first step is opening your mind to the possibility that maybe your evenings of cold pizza and rented movies will soon be over. Don't let bitterness or fear of disappointment stand between you and a new love. This is a new adventure. Accept that you might find a partner and be open to it.

Look at Yourself as a Product

"Me? A product?" you ask. "A living, breathing person is not a commodity that can be bought with a limited time, 30 percent off coupon or two-for-one discount." However, to successfully market yourself you must think of yourself in those terms. It will allow you to be more objective. If you have trouble thinking of yourself as a product, pretend you're a fine bottle of imported champagne rather than the latest fad beer or a fully equipped, luxury Porsche rather than the new compact economy car. Another way is to think of one-of-a-kind products, like real estate or a rare collectible. Doing this will help you to see the parallels in product marketing more clearly.

Force Yourself

A successful job search requires that you get out there and talk to people. The same is true for finding a partner. You can't allow loneliness, depression, and the resulting low self-esteem to keep you out of circulation. Even a bad experience will probably not be as bad as you may imagine. And every positive experience will build your confidence.

Commit to the Process and Then Persevere

Don't expect to run a personal ad only once and reach your goal. Toyota doesn't. Pepsi doesn't. So you shouldn't either. It may take several ads before you're pleased with the results. You may have to refine your copy—or run your ad in a different publication. You may find that your goals have changed. You'll find that once you've placed an ad, following up with the responses takes time. So you'll need to make your dating life a priority to benefit from our process.

Keep Doing What You Love

Do you love playing tennis, reading, going to movies, or painting? Hobbies build our self-esteem. Keep doing the hobbies and activities that make you happy. When you focus on yourself, not on finding the perfect mate, you'll approach the dating game with more energy, confidence, and attitude, enabling you to come across as more attractive. Besides, whether you run personal ads or not, you must remember that your perfect match can turn up when and where you least expect it. Be alert. And don't quit getting dates from other means.

Take It Step-by-Step

Using the personals isn't like placing an ad for a used sofa or a '71 Nova. A personal ad can change your life. It can help you broaden your horizons, make new friends—and even introduce you to your future spouse. So it's important to do it right.

This book provides direction on creating effective personal ads based on classic advertising and marketing principles—principles used by the world's top companies to market their brands. You'll learn how to target your message by figuring out what type of relationship you want, who you want, what you have to offer, and how to use language to communicate these needs. You'll also learn how to choose the media options that will work best for you. You'll have expert advice on how to protect yourself while dating. And you'll read ads by people who've found successful relationships through the personals, which happens more often than you may think.

Will it ever be happily ever after? Just like any other couple, you'll never know for sure . . . that is, until you're past your 50th anniversary. But your chances for success along the journey are the same as if you met your partner at a singles party or a bar—or through work, friends, relatives, or just on the street in a random encounter.

So give it a try, and, meanwhile, *enjoy the ride.*

A Special Note to Women

Quit thinking all the nice men are married or gay. The man shortage has sold a lot of books and magazines. But statistics are irrelevant because they cannot predict any individual's odds for finding a mate. A singles magazine in San Francisco prints more than 800 personal ads every month. But you don't need all 800 of them. You need just one. So even if there is a shortage, there's no reason you shouldn't be able to find the partner you want. Just go to it!

From *Playmates*
to *Playpens*

Every lover I ever married turned out to be a wife.

—Michael Brown, poet

Before you even begin to think about which 25 words or less you should use to write an ad, invest in a dating service, or start flirting with someone in a bar, you should figure out what kind of a relationship you want. If you clarify the level of commitment and intimacy you desire—at least in the short-term—you won't waste your time on people who aren't suited to you. And you won't become involved with a person who has a different agenda than yours.

Take Valerie, a friendly, outgoing 31-year-old who works in a CPA firm. Her personality and good looks have helped her meet dozens of men in bars. She dated many of them, but prefers to use the personals because they allow her an opportunity to target the type of men she wants to meet. She placed this ad in a suburban newspaper:

> **BULLS, BEARS, BEER** Now that I have your attention this SWF, 31, 5'9" brown/brown, is looking for you, an attractive, tall SWM 30–36, who likes to have fun. For more info, call . . .

Valerie received about 15 responses. Many of them came from men who seemed very nice. She met Rob, a recently divorced father of two. He was attractive, kind, and nurturing. She liked him. He liked her. And for about seven months, they enjoyed a great relationship. But Valerie began to want more of a commitment. Rob wasn't ready for marriage so soon after his divorce. So they broke up. If Valerie had stated her desire for an eventual long-term commitment, she might have avoided heartbreak and found someone who was more open to her goal.

Like Valerie's, your ad may attract a lot of nice people. Some may be looking for marriage. Some may only want to date. You need to be clear about your expectations. Knowing the type of relationship you want helps you to be more selective. For instance, if you're looking for marriage, you may want to target people who are clearly ready for this commitment. While this may reduce the overall number of responses you get, you'll probably attract people who are a better match for you. If, on the other hand, you decide that you just want a period of dating and to expand your circle of friends, you'll want a larger number of responses from a broader range of people. In other words, identifying the type of relationship you want will help you plan an effective strategy, driving where you place your ad as well as what you say.

In this chapter, we will present several types of common relationships that we identified based on our interviews with people who use the personals. But keep in mind that relationships can be found across a spectrum, not pigeonholed into a category. The more specific you can be in describing the type of relationship you want to develop, the more likely it becomes that you'll reach your goal. To help you define the level of involvement that you're seeking in a relationship, ask yourself:

- Do you want to be able to go to his or her house without calling first?
- Do you want to meet his or her friends? Do you want this person to meet your friends?
- Do you want to meet your partner's parents and/or children? Have this person meet your parents or children?
- Do you want to be invited to family events? Holidays? Birthdays?
- Do you want to include him or her at your business gatherings? Be included at his or her business gatherings?

- Do you want to answer each other's telephone?
- Are you looking for a one-night stand?
- Do you want a monogamous sexual relationship?
- How quickly would you want a sexual relationship?
- Do you want to spend the night at each other's house? After how long?
- Do you want to go on vacations together?
- Do you want to live together?
- Do you want to have a joint checking account?
- Do you want to help him or her with the household chores?
- Do you want to have a child (or children) with him or her?

All of these questions fall into five common types of relationships. In this chapter we'll explore the different types to help you identify the one you want. But before you start reading the sections, ask yourself:

- Do I want to expand my circle of friends?
- Do I want dating mania?
- Do I want a sexual friendship?
- Do I want a steady relationship?
- Do I want to live happily ever after?

If you clearly know the type of relationship you want, go to that specific section and review it. Make sure that's what you really want. If so, great; you're ahead of the game. But if not, it's OK. Part of the dating process is to learn about yourself and your relationships, so you become more focused.

What's more, remember that motives evolve. You may think you know what you want and then change your mind later. For instance, look at Peter. He had been dating through the personals off and on for approximately seven years when he placed the following ad:

Seeking quality, not quantity time! Tall, fit, charming, creative SWM, 32, seeks confident, fit, engaging SDF, 22–42, for something halfway between diversion and "I do." If you have an interesting, demanding life with a midsized hole in it shaped like a romantic, progressive, straightforward person, let's complete the puzzle together. Write . . .

Preferring mail over a phone message, he received two written responses. He met the first woman for lunch and realized immediately that she wasn't for him. "She just had different interests than I did," he said. The second response was from Claira. She wrote him a letter and said she would like him to write back. He did and they traded three letters each before they finally met. (See Chapter 7 for reprinted letters.) "I was immediately taken with her from her letters," he said. "She seemed excited about life and the world." So a week and a half after finally meeting face-to-face, while they were on a date to celebrate his birthday, he told her that he had become interested in a more committed relationship. But she wasn't ready for a commitment—at least not yet. Not for a long time. She was 10 years younger than he, was just finishing up graduate school, and wanted some time just to experience life on her own.

But they continued dating—and Peter also started seeing another woman he had met through the personals (she had responded to a different ad that he'd placed in a competing publication). Wendy was 30, blond, and interested in alternative music. She had a caustic sense of humor. Whenever he'd try to compliment Wendy, she'd respond, "Yeah, right." But when he finally became intimate with Claira (about five weeks after he'd begun dating the other woman), he broke up with Wendy (who eventually went back to her ex-boyfriend). "I realized that it wasn't going to work because I had strong feelings for Claira," he said. And the new turn in their relationship created "enough of a commitment" for him. They continued dating and Claira eventually decided that she too wanted a more committed relationship. They got engaged, waited a year for their wedding, married, and at the time of this writing had already celebrated their first wedding anniversary.

Peter realized that his change in motive might have caused some of the problems early in their relationship. "The point is not to fool people into answering your ad," he said of his experience. "The point is to represent yourself positively and accurately and hope that others respond in kind."

But his ad gave him a starting point. And you need a starting point, too. So let's begin with the least commitment and continue to the most legally binding—marriage. We'll also cover one type that you might not have thought of but is equally valid: no relationship at all—at least for now.

Do I Want to Expand My Circle of Friends?

In our research we learned about high-powered executives with little time to meet a man or woman through traditional methods. Some were transferred by their megaconglomerate corporations to a new town. Others held to strict rules against engaging in office romances (generally a good idea, but dating people from your professional life can be a great way to meet a future spouse). We also talked with college students who wanted to expand their horizons beyond the campus. And we heard from a recent divorcée whose ex got custody of their friends.

So if you've spent every waking hour developing a career, that could be why you are not married. That could be why all of your coworkers have spouses and children with braces and you have a corner office that you inhabit even on weekends. Cultivating—and maintaining—a loving, caring relationship takes work, and you've spent your time cultivating your career instead. You might even be thinking that if your coworkers invited you out once in a while, you probably wouldn't enjoy socializing with them much anyway.

But everyone needs a few friendships—someone to look in on you now and again, someone, at least, besides your mother. That way, the next time you fall in your shower and break your leg, you won't have to worry about lying there until your rent comes due (to borrow the words of one overly concerned parent).

But you don't have to be transferred by your corporation, totally focused on building your career, or newly divorced to need new friendships. Some time around age 22, many people begin to feel like a fifth wheel because all their friends have become significantly attached, married, had children, and prefer the company of other couples. Even if the single friend is still included, an evening at the theater must now be coordinated by a cast of thousands—husbands, wives, grandparents, babysitters, and whoever has a car that fits everyone. Somehow trying to play becomes too much work.

In this life stage, you may long for the days of spontaneity—for friends you can call up on a Wednesday night and invite to the movies. You don't want to understand why conversations always have to involve mortgage rates and day-care policies (at least, just yet). And you don't want to be interrupted constantly by your friend's child asking for help or a snack.

If any of what we just said strikes a chord with you, then you may find that personal ads give you a great opportunity to meet a lot of people without a lot of work. Just type up your ad, send it in to your local newspaper (or use another media option; see Chapter 5), and you'll be on your way to developing new friends.

But expanding your circle of friends is a good strategy for another reason: it may help you eventually find a marriage partner. Don't expect to find a mate immediately through the ads; just enjoy developing a wide circle of close friends right now. Then over time, see if one of those friendships blossoms into something more (or see if he or she will introduce you to one of his or her single friends). That's the strategy Carl used.

Carl ran an ad and received dozens of responses. He tried to decide too quickly who was right for him. He wound up with two relationships that lasted only a few months. At that point, he felt that it was too late for him to contact any of the other women who had responded. So months later, he ran the ad on the following page and vowed to contact as many respondents as possible and develop as many new friendships as possible before establishing a monogamous relationship.

Carl received over 100 responses to this ad. Is he living happily ever after? No, because he found that trying to handle the large volume of responses that he had generated put him at a disadvantage. He is still trying to sort through the many responses. He plans to approach this task as a process; in the first phone conversation, he'll weed out respondents he feels would be incompatible. Then he'll spend a lot of time becoming friends with the remainder, so he will get to know them more thoroughly before developing any romantic ties. (For those of you who don't want to take the time to develop your own process, see Chapter 8 for our suggestions.)

SWM, 32, celebrated birthday sky diving (head case). I'm good-looking (who isn't in these ads), creative (wrote a poem in second grade), slim (skinny), athletic (can walk and chew gum) who likes taking risks and believes that my dreams can come true (lives in a fantasy world). I enjoy helping people (compassionate), rain tennis (goofball), playing with my nephews (family man), and laughing with friends about the absurdities of life in the 90s (this ad). I've gotten over the pain of ending a 3-year relationship (rebound) and now find myself excited (desperate) about the prospect of having someone new in my life (to stomp on my heart). I'm very nurturing and love being nurtured in return (I rub your back, you rub mine). The way to my heart is definitely through my stomach (if you cook, I'll do the dishes). My dream (delusion) is to have us build a strong friendship that will evolve into a lifelong commitment ("M word," "M word"). To find out more about me, my dear, put pen to paper or phone to ear.

Even if you want a committed, monogamous relationship, expanding your circle of friends is a great way to find it. By developing a friendship first, you'll find out if your potential partner is a liar, alcoholic, drug addict, compulsive gambler, or simply a messed up person—*before* your life becomes totally entangled with his or hers.

Do I Want Dating Mania?

Are you recently divorced and the ink on the papers hasn't dried yet? Do you occasionally embarrass yourself by referring to your ex as your husband or wife? Do you still feel naked without a wedding ring? If so, you're probably not ready for another relationship. These are signs that you shouldn't try settling down just yet.

If you do you'll probably walk into the same sort of relationship because that's all you know; it feels right and you haven't sorted out the issues that made your first relationship fall apart. You don't have to watch *Oprah* every day or participate in the latest John Bradshaw seminar to know that neurotic family dynamics can perpetuate themselves generation after generation. Wouldn't it be nice to experiment? Meet and date a variety of people? Watch yourself change and grow in the context of many relationships . . . or at least in the context of another person's neurotic family dynamics?

There are other reasons you may not be ready to be in a committed or monogamous relationship quite yet. Maybe you were out of commission for a while because you were in the middle of an ocean on a Navy ship. Maybe you were focused on a huge project for your employer. Or maybe you're just craving variety in your life. Whatever the reason, dating lots of people may be just what you need.

Later in this book we'll meet people who took this strategy. If it's for you as well, watch for their ads and look at their results and use them as a guide when you develop your ad.

There are people who think that they fall into another category but really belong in this one. Take John, for example. He *thought* he was marriage minded when he ran this ad:

> SWM, 42, attorney, 6'0" 175 lbs., blue eyes, active with a wide variety of interests, marriage minded, and interested in children, seeks affectionate, self-reliant, college-educated nonsmoker. Ages 25–35 preferred.

He placed this ad and received a handful of responses, but after a few dates he realized that maybe he'd been out of circulation longer than he'd thought. The dating world had changed and he needed time to catch up. None of his dates was a success; he was even stood up by one date in a bar. "I don't get it," he said. "I'm an attorney. I have to deal with people every day. I'm presentable, personable. I don't have big boils growing out of my head."

If he ever runs another ad, what will he do differently? Move the age bracket up? Place an ad in a publication whose readers are a little more settled, not the off-the-wall newspaper that he used? Be more creative? "Nah," said Phil, "I'm not really creative. Why pretend?"

Will he be more specific about interests or hobbies? "Nah. I don't care if a woman likes to go in-line skating or eat ethnic food. I care more about honesty, kindness, and a good personality." In the meantime, he hopes to meet and date as many different women as possible; recently he met a flight attendant who wants to get together with him again. This one, he says, seems promising.

Do I Want a Sexual Friendship?

Maybe what you want is a sexual friendship—a casual but ongoing sexual relationship with a companion. These relationships seem to "just happen" when people have no time or inclination for commitment. Sometimes they happen because people are lonely.

Rarely does anyone set out with this type of relationship in mind. Typically, a couple goes out on a few dates. They like each other enough. They are attracted to each other. But for some reason, they don't see themselves as a couple with potential for a long-term relationship. So, they openly agree to look for the mate of their dreams and remain sexually involved. If one partner should begin seriously dating someone new, the other steps aside. At worst, he or she may sulk for a day.

Peter, whom we met near the beginning of this chapter, had just such a sexual companion. She was three years older than he, attractive, and intelligent. He met her when he responded to one of her ads, and they dated for a summer before they broke up.

But they remained friends and, when neither of them was in a serious relationship, they'd sleep together. finally, he realized that this was not working for him. "I decided that this was crazy," he said. "We weren't in love. So there was no reason to be doing this, because clearly, we didn't have a romantic future together." When he stopped sleeping with her (they remained friends), he opened himself up to the possibilities of meeting someone new and he decided to place the ad that resulted in his meeting Claira (and you know the rest!).

So what about people having extramarital affairs? Well, they are different from sexual friends in a number of important ways. They rarely admit that their relationships have no future. They often indulge in expectations, and their relationships are almost always based on deceit. How can you believe in someone who has broken a solemn vow made to someone else? What's keeping this person from breaking promises made to you as well? The question will always be there. And when the affair ends, the resulting disappointment and anger typically do not allow the people involved to maintain any sort of friendship.

Uncommitted boyfriends or girlfriends also differ from sexual friends. You don't take a sexual companion to your family reunion or grandmother's birthday—or anywhere you might meet your real match. Swingers are also in a different category, as they don't cultivate a deep friendship, or limit their sexual activities to the same person. Sexual friends are not just using each other. They enjoy each other's company and hope the best for each other. Their open communication fosters a deep friendship. They can afford to be open. They have nothing to lose.

The advantage of having a sexual friendship is obvious: regular sex with no commitment. Plus, because the relationship is so open, it's usually safer sex because both partners know where the other has been. They're less shy about birth control and using condoms with nonoxynol-9.

Can sexual friendships turn into happily ever after? Maybe if you're both stranded on a desert island for a few decades. Or buried in a mine shaft with only a limited air supply. Or someday you realize that your brand of true love doesn't cause the fireworks you were brought up to believe in.

How do you place an ad for this type of relationship? Forget it. Although some people try, as we said at the beginning of this section, the best sexual friendship just happens, generally evolving out of an existing friendship or casual dating relationship. Just know it when you see it.

Do I Want a Steady Relationship?

Do you engage in so much small talk that you're considering writing all relevant data about your life on a piece of paper and handing it out on dates? Do you want to order tickets to a Japanese Kabuki rendition of *Oklahoma!*, but you're not sure who you could talk into going with you? Do you fear entering contests where the prize is a vacation for two because if you won you'd have to bring a relative for companionship? Do your cats know you better than anyone else? Then perhaps you want a steady relationship.

The stability of a steady relationship can help you make plans. You can start using a pen to write entries in your calendar.

But there are a wide variety of steady relationships. When you're young, your steady is referred to as your boyfriend or girlfriend. When you're older, your steady is the longtime companion. Other terms include *old man, old lady, squeeze,* and *appendage.*

Steady couples may see each other once a week or every day. Some live together. Some couples are very much in love; others are cool about their passions. Some have everything but a marriage license; others have nothing more than a regular meal together at their favorite Tibetan restaurant. So if you feel you've dated enough people and you've got two tickets for a cruise, you may want to start looking for a steady relationship. That's what Megan wanted when she wrote the following ad:

> No more games. Quirky, sensitive, attractive 31 y.o. SWF seeks an introspective, sincere, unpretentious male (W/H, 30–38) who enjoys the treasures of Chicago, yet appreciates the great outdoors.

Megan was pleased with her 18 responses, finding the one from an attorney particularly intriguing. She made a date to meet him. The trouble was, throughout their meeting she was totally distracted by the man's blackened teeth. As of this writing, she plans on following up on the other responses she received. Perhaps one of them will turn into a steady relationship.

Do I Want to Live Happily Ever After?

You've already pressed the snooze button on your biological clock—for the third time. You need a green card. You're afraid of choking on your food and you want someone around who knows the Heimlich maneuver. Or maybe you want to find someone to love you well into your old age. All of these fall into the category of happily ever after.

Yes, it can happen. You can meet someone through the personal ads and like him or her enough to want to see him or her every morning before either of you brush your teeth . . . for the rest of your life. Just look at Peter and Claira. Or the couple who inspired Sally from Chapter 1 to try the personals. Many people have found successful, loving, committed relationships through the personals. It happens more often than you may think.

Do I Really Want a Relationship At All?

As you probably realize, having another person in your life isn't always easy—especially in the beginning of a relationship. If all the considerations above have caused more confusion than insight, maybe you're not quite ready to accommodate the schedule, expectations, and emotions of another person. And while a personal ad can attract someone whose needs are similar to yours, it's OK not to want a relationship at all. You may decide that you're at a time of your life when you relish your solitude and privacy; the chance to spend time doing exactly what you want to do. That's fine.

Sam realized this while he was trying to find a woman to replace his ex-wife soon after his divorce. The break-up had been particularly hard on him because he grew up in a conservative Bible-reading family. After the ninth grade, he was home-schooled. At age 15 he'd met his ex-wife, a plain girl who shared his values and commitment to the Bible. She'd grown up even more sheltered than he. "It was almost an Amish environment," he said. He married her after she turned 18—sincere in the belief that he was making a lifetime commitment. They had a daughter. Slowly, however, his wife began loosening up. Using makeup. Wearing sexy clothes. Wanting more "fun" money.

Sam broadened his views to maintain their relationship. He felt that his commitment was being tested. But his wife spent more and more time in front of the mirror. Heads began to turn when she walked down the street. The attention encouraged her to push her limits even further. Sam struggled harder to do everything he could to please her.

Then came the late nights out. Other men. She even got a job as a stripper. And she filed for divorce. Sam felt that in trying to save their relationship he'd compromised his values.

The experience had caused this 26-year-old to put considerable thought into what he wanted in a relationship. So six months out of their five-year marriage, he decided to place an ad on-line. He knew the computer world, and it offered enough space for him to communicate his thoughts. He wrote an approximately 1,800-word letter (eight double-spaced pages) detailing the type of relationship he wanted. It started:

> *Dear Future Wife,*
> *May this letter reach you in best of health!*
> *I am sending this letter to all of you women in the WORLD whose eyes this message has reached. My views are not popular, I will tell you that! I am looking for a particular woman who knows, as I feel I do, that the meaning of life is love, work, commitment, and family. Balancing my beliefs, I am a very gentle, loving, understanding, strong, and sensitive man. If you do not like what I say here, that is OK. You are entitled to your own choices.*
> *I could start off this message with my physical statistics, but I will not. My physical characteristics are ultimately inconsequential to the kind of woman I am looking for, so I choose to leave them out, as it serves as a "filter" right off for what is unacceptable.*
> *Important are a couple of areas that need to be discussed distinctly and I may go into more detail in some than others. The main areas are: Our Marriage, Family, and Future.*
> *You can choose to call some of these things "rules," expectations, or you may just choose to view them as they are, "guiding boundaries" of respect, true love, comfort, and security.*

In his letter, he said he'd be the breadwinner; that his wife would run the household and raise any children; and he'd set the "rules" and that his wife would follow them. He concluded his letter by writing:

> *Let me ask you a question — point blank. Is capturing my heart something that you can take or leave — or is it something that you're smart enough to really want?*

You do not wait until you find out I am worth millions, or have my house built and paid for, or see my tanned washboard stomach. You start this relationship now.

Come to me and feel safe in the security of your shield: me. You are smart; when the time comes you are capable of finding me.

— Sam

Whether you share Sam's fairly rigid definition of an ideal marriage or not, you must admit that the 1,800 words enabled him to communicate his expectations for a relationship. In fact, he did such a good job that his letter inspired more than 50 responses from a wide range of people.

Although Sam did receive a few hate letters, many friendlier letters, filled with support and encouragement, also poured in from married women. They wrote about frustrations with husbands who couldn't hold jobs, didn't spend time with their children, and didn't respect them. "Like the song, where have all the cowboys gone?" said one response, perhaps misreading Paula Cole's sarcastic hit song about the inability to find an old-fashioned love, where the man goes off drinking every night and the woman stays home to wash the dishes. Others asked, "Where were you when I married 12 years ago?" Sam felt so sad for them that he'd find himself on the verge of tears when reading their letters. Younger women, from ages 18 to their late 20s, told him they were interested and shared their stories.

But Sam was most moved by the numerous letters from divorced mothers in their thirties. Many were beautiful, well-educated women. They wrote of their struggles to care for their children, their grief over failed marriages, and their frustrations in dealing with wishy-washy, noncommittal men. And although they were older, Sam's experiences were most similar to theirs. Sam started e-mail dialogue with many of them. "They captured my heart," he says. "In a way, I fell in love with each one of them."

The support he received affirmed his belief in his values and caused him to end his search. He wrote all the women he had corresponded with, thanked them for their care, and told them he was no longer interested.

Sam decided that looking for a second wife went against everything he believed in. His vows had said, "Till death do us part." No legal papers could undo Sam's commitment. That doesn't mean he needs to expose himself to his ex-wife's behavior but that he should remain alone. The wonderful women who responded could only expect a secondhand commitment from him—and Sam felt they, and he, deserved more. Sam is beginning to have happier times with friends. He's determined to let the future take care of itself. And, for now, he feels peaceful with his decision to remain alone.

Like Sam, other personal-ad users have learned that, after placing ads and receiving responses, they didn't really want to commit their time to a relationship. They had placed the ads in a burst of desperation. They had felt if they didn't find a partner soon, their odds would dwindle and they'd spend their old age lonely and miserable.

Receiving responses reassured them that there were plenty of decent possibilities out there. That reality helped them overcome their fears of being unattached. They learned that when they were ready to pursue romance, there would be people who were interested. And because ads can work for people of all ages, there's no hurry.

In *Are You the One for Me?*, relationship guru Barbara DeAngelis explored some of the *wrong* reasons people look for love. Social pressure is a common motivation for seeking a relationship, because our society is very couple oriented. But the need for another person should come from within yourself, not from the awkwardness felt by attending a wedding stag.

Other people use relationships to distract them from their own lives. They avoid going back to school or looking for a new job when they make finding another person a priority. In some cases, people lean on a partner to avoid growing up. It's easier to escape independent, responsible behavior when there's someone to lean on. Emotional or spiritual emptiness can spur one to seek fulfillment and purpose in others as well. So when should one look for a relationship? As DeAngelis suggests, when you feel full of love and want to share it.

After reading this chapter, you may have decided that your circumstances are unique. Perhaps you're gay. Or you may be one half of a couple looking for someone to warm the extra space on the king-sized bed. Or you simply want someone to sunbathe in the nude with you on your yacht. And you're whining to yourself because we haven't addressed your special interests.

Now, now. All the above relationships can also describe the needs of gays, couples, or people involved in less traditional lifestyles. A gay man or woman could want a lifetime mate or a steady date. One couple looking for a third party may want a much deeper relationship than would another couple.

Also, there may be other types of relationships we haven't mentioned. There's a broad spectrum and no way to foresee every possible need. But every ad is designed to achieve something specific. And its success is judged by how close it comes to achieving its intended results. Your first step in developing an effective personal ad is knowing exactly what you want to achieve. We recommend starting with the categories we've described, but then get even more focused and specific. Once you've identified the type of relationship you want, simply write it out on a piece of paper.

In the following chapters, we will show you how to use the personal ads to get what you want. Just remember the old proverb: "Be careful what you wish for, because you just may get it." Be prepared.

All About *You*

We are shaped and fashioned by what we love.

—*Goethe*

Mark, a 39-year-old, gay, HIV-positive software writer had heard about people meeting through the personals and thought that this arena was only for people who couldn't meet someone any other way. But when encephalitis caused him to become paralyzed, his social life became paralyzed as well. Plus, he'd just moved from New Orleans to Richmond, Virginia, and didn't know too many people.

Mark's parents wanted to see him boost his social life and urged him to use the computer to meet new people on-line. He initially rejected their advice, but eventually he gave in, figuring that anyone who could cough up $2,000 for a computer might just have something to offer him.

At first, Mark simply browsed the Internet, which he found to be boring. But then he loaded America Online and began visiting chat rooms. In no time Mark was addicted—spending as much as 10 hours a day on-line—and his social life showed it. He looked at profiles of other people and sent a message if he was interested. He also created a profile and Web page for himself and sent the Web address to interested members. It read:

```
      Member Name:  Mark
         Location:  Richmond, VA
        Birthdate:  6/16/58
              Sex:  Male
   Marital Status:  Not sure right now
          Hobbies:  Weightlifting, movies,
                    theater, symphony, dining
        Computers:  Very funny, Scotty.
                    Now beam up my clothes.
       Occupation:  Semi-retired—work as volunteer
                    full time with AIDS patients
   Personal Quote:  Living with HIV.
```

While he was e-mailing his photo to others whose profiles interested him and building his list of virtual friends, he was also getting well and building up his strength. Today, Mark is back to work—and still socializing on-line. His list has grown to 80 members, and he has established two good friendships.

A few on-line friendships turned into face-to-face meetings. Sometimes the men he met didn't want a relationship with someone who was HIV positive. In those cases, Mark reminded the person to be careful. He knew from experience that many people who know they're HIV positive won't admit it to a potential partner. Other times, the dates understood how to minimize the risk and were open to the possibility of a relationship with him. This included Joel, whom Mark met in a chat room. It didn't take long for them to exchange photos, share stories, and discover they were both looking for a long-term relationship. After dating for more than a month, Mark feels there's potential.

Most people were surprised that Mark was so open about being HIV positive, but he thought it was easier and more fair to both parties to know all the facts up front. His directness saved him time and opened the door to meeting others. Sometimes he got e-mail from people who were diagnosed as HIV positive and needed help.

"I used to laugh about the caliber of people who dated through ads or computers," he said, "but I was so wrong. Now I wouldn't do it any other way."

Why was Mark so successful? Because he recognized the need to be honest, up front, and specific about all of his attributes. Like Mark, to write a great ad about yourself, you need to take some time to understand who you really are—both physically and emotionally—and to find, in marketing terms, your "unique selling proposition," a phrase originated by the advertising executive Rosser Reeves in his classic book *Reality in Advertising.* Using this concept in the 1950s and 1960s, Rosser Reeves's agency—Ted Bates & Company—created tons of effective advertising campaigns. From M&M's ("It melts in your mouth, not in your hand") to Colgate ("It cleans your breath, as it cleans your teeth"), each campaign recognized that the product it was promoting offered a unique benefit to its audience. And each campaign was highly effective. So please take your time with this step, because not only will getting your unique attributes written down on paper help you maintain clarity when you meet someone, it will help you when you write your ad.

True, you may be thinking, "I'm fun, intelligent, sensitive, and disease free. Writing a personal ad for myself should be simple. What's the big deal? All I have to do is write down a few adjectives like *attractive, successful,* and *warm.* Right?" Well, yes, that's fine if you want a generic-sounding ad (and perfect if you're a generic human being). But a truly successful personal ad, one that will generate better-quality responses, eliminate later work, and help protect against later heartache, will take more effort than that.

The best ads are specific in communicating the attributes of the product, service, job position, or, in this case, person being advertised. For example, imagine an over-the-counter drug being sold with only "fast-acting" and "quick relief" on the label. Those are positive things, but they don't say what the drug is for; what it does; what age group it's intended for; or what precautions should be taken when using it. These questions need to be answered before someone will want to try the drug. Or just imagine an ad for that same medicine simply saying that it will make you feel "really good." That would be irresponsible advertising, yet many personal ads fail to say much more than that.

If you overlook the process of discovering what you're all about, your label will be just as vague. Why should anyone believe and act on your ad? Remember, we're living in an age of skepticism, if not fear, and cocooning. Specifics are what create credibility and make you real. So you need to identify your desirable qualities clearly as well as identify the characteristics that your target may not find appealing.

Doing this will not only help you figure out the content of your ad (the words), it will help you identify its tone (whether you should be serious or fun or ironic), as well as where to place it once it's been written.

Think of it this way: to sell a car, the marketing executive must first thoroughly know the product—the style, the engine's capabilities, the production time, the distribution channels, the cost, and many other features. This will enable the executive to create the most effective plan as well as talk articulately about its features and benefits.

The marketing executive must also understand the consumer audience because successful marketing identifies the consumers' needs or wants and then communicates a message that shows consumers how the product will fulfill them. And because people are so varied in their needs, interests, and personalities, marketers offer a range of styles and technical variations.

Let's use the analogy of a new car. In terms of selling the car, identifying and fulfilling the consumers' wants and needs means tweaking the product, perhaps adding safety features or horsepower or developing a new model altogether. But once a car is ready for sale, the important task is to create the perception that its attributes will appeal to a specific type of person (which the product advertising has been designed to target). If the product's message is filled with false promises, its popularity will be short-lived. If, on the other hand, it misses its target, even a great product can fail. Communicating a positive, believable message is the key to success.

So part of your job in creating a personal ad is to find what's unique to you that will appeal to your target (not as a feature but as a benefit).

For an example of the magic of a unique selling proposition, consider the Pet Rock. Back in the 1970s, someone actually had the audacity to place a common rock among a few strands of straw in a quaintly decorated box and sell it to the public as a pet—all for about the price of a dinner out. The Pet Rock was a huge success. They were sold in bookstores, gift shops, drugstores, and many other retail stores.

The product responded to our need to own a pet (this one was positioned as being maintenance free), share humor, encounter novelty, and be frivolous. In many ways, the product succeeded in doing those things—which accounted for its popularity. But in fulfilling the deeper need to nurture and bond with a pet, it failed—which (along with the fact that it stopped being novel) accounted for its quick demise.

Now imagine hearing the inventor of the Pet Rock describe this product. Imagine asking a bank to invest in it. Imagine the confidence that was needed to make the Pet Rock into the fad that it became. And like the Pet Rock, there have been dozens of other incredibly popular products whose success is largely due to enhanced image, or perception, rather than actual value. Your popularity also depends on the image—or personal style—you project.

Here's a great ad that has more style than substance. It was written by Steve, a 24-year-old student. Since he was working his way through school, he had little time for socializing. And the people he met weren't the kind of people he enjoyed hanging out with. So he decided to put his poetry and songwriting talents to use and came up with this ad:

Cooler Man . . . handsome man, ransom man, have some man . . .
rasta man, non-pasta man, lotsa man, hotsa man . . .
stylin' man, flyin' man, try this man, can't buy this man . . .
diesel man, feel this man, steal this man, don't deal this man . . .
drummer man, summer man, the cooler man, the cooler man,
the cooler man . . .

Although he didn't say much about himself, he did communicate an attitude—and that attitude inspired responses from several women. Then, when they called his voice-mail number, they got all the vital information about Steve and his interests. So, as you can see, he still had to conduct some form of self-assessment and communicate his attributes to the potential dates; he just let his personal style and attitude play a bigger role up front, implying that he had a sense of fun (perhaps his biggest attribute).

You might be thinking that marketing a product is different than marketing a person. But think about all the entertainers and politicians who rise to the top—even though we all know that they don't have the character and/or the brains to deserve the positions they hold. Think of your boss perhaps . . . now do you believe us? Often the biggest difference between us and a more successful person is that he or she succeeded in selling his or her value—or worthiness—to a greater number of people. Of course, there are job requirements, special talents, and qualifications that must be met to attain certain positions. Yet, as we know from politics, what one communicates about oneself often separates the successful candidate from the rest of the equally qualified people. We're not suggesting an advertising campaign that is as challenging—and as expensive—as running for senator. Or as content-void as a Pepsi commercial, which sells itself through the imagery it projects. Your goal is simply to find a companion.

But as Dr. Judy Kuriansky wrote in *The Complete Idiot's Guide to Dating,* "People are drawn to people who like themselves. Self-confidence screams sex appeal."

Likewise, no characteristic is as unattractive as low self-esteem. That's one of the most important lessons you may learn from using the personals. Bob did. He was a single, 34-year-old, college-educated, financially responsible, polished, creative guy who had a great sense of humor. He had many good friends, worked as a professional opera singer and had another full-time job in a sales office. Yet Bob didn't believe that he was attractive, so he used personal ads to meet women. He felt that, unlike a bar, personal ads allowed him to first introduce his most appealing characteristics. And, because he valued honesty, he didn't lie about his height, weight, and hair—or lack thereof. Here was his ad:

> Show business professional, 34, 5′7″,
> Jason Alexander type. An examined life and
> pleasing wit. Derived joy from martinis before they were
> popular, prefers Sammy to Frank and is amused by the
> resurgence of lime green. Seeks SWF, ns, who
> considers sparkling conversation and humor an
> asset, for adventure and frolic.

Bob chose to compare himself to Jason Alexander (who plays George on *Seinfeld*) because of the physical similarities and because Alexander was so popular. Bob then focused on his core interests and the qualities that he wanted in a prospective partner. (And, as you can see his ad didn't include adjectives like *attractive, slim,* or *petite.*)

Bob received up to six responses each time he ran his ad, and since he was seeking a serious relationship, that was enough to keep him busy. The trouble was, he felt that the women who contacted him did so not for his positive qualities, but because they suspected that his physique would make him less choosy. And although he didn't state any physical requirements, he was very particular about finding someone whose polished style, values, and interests matched his own.

The important role Bob's own insecurities played in his quest were driven home when he met Diana. Diana was a high school music teacher with an interest in opera who responded with a phone message. Though she lived an hour away from Bob's urban quarters, their rapport was so positive and their interests so parallel that she was willing to meet him.

Bob arrived at Diana's favorite restaurant dressed in one of his finely tailored suits. Having met through the personals, he felt confident that her interest in him was not based on superficial qualities—which bolstered his confidence even further. And when Diana arrived, he discovered a Greek beauty. They had a wonderful dinner. Later, they used her key to a nearby university's theater to demonstrate their musical talents to each other in the dimly lit, empty house. It was a dream date.

They continued to date and, several weeks later, Bob was shocked to learn that Diana had never read his ad that contained his physical description. She had merely heard his message while browsing through the voice-mail system. Bob realized that if he'd known that she was unaware of his appearance, he would never have approached the first meeting feeling so confident. He was the one who made an issue of his looks. His own insecurities, not his appearance, were getting in his way. It was his confidence that made him so attractive to Diana.

A similar phenomenon is described by Leil Lowndes in *How to Make Anyone Fall in Love with You.* The author was captivated by a TV newsmagazine's experiment proving that attractiveness paid off. The show sent two women—one perceived as attractive, the other perceived as unattractive—to run out of gas in different cars of the same make and model. Typically, the attractive woman had no trouble finding a good samaritan to assist her. The less attractive woman only encountered one man who said he'd have someone return to help her. The puzzling aspect of the experiment, according to the author, was her observation that the two women did not greatly differ in appearance. Both were of similar height, weight, facial features, and hair color and style. So what was the difference that caused one woman to be perceived as unattractive? She leaned against the car, arms folded across her chest, looking miserable and unsure of herself. The "attractive" woman flung back her hair with a wave of her head and appeared positive, hopeful, and confident.

So believing that—and then acting like—you're desirable to the opposite sex helps. And while you may obsess about how you'll never find a partner because of your receding hairline or spreading thighs, the biggest objection you'll have to overcome is the negative thoughts in your own mind. In fact, low expectations can inhibit happiness far more than any of the narrow prerequisites of a potential partner. But your belief in yourself is what will give you the confidence and courage to make a strong statement on your own behalf. As every successful salesperson knows, this is what gives your message conviction and makes you more effective.

But while having healthy self-esteem is the first step, it also helps if you keep your ego in check. It's true that while many of us need to learn how to drown out inner voices that echo our insecurities, others need to tame inflated egos.

These people often look good on paper. They're physically attractive. They're intelligent. They enjoy a comfortable lifestyle. They recognize these gifts as desirable and they make sure that their personal ad shines with every stellar detail. They advertise in expensive publications and insist on a high level of attractiveness or income or both from respondents.

This doesn't mean that all successful people have big egos. It just means that if you make yourself sound too good to be true, you may be revealing an ego problem, because—as in any ad—if something sounds too good to be true, it probably is.

But why deflate good feelings when it's so important to think well of ourselves? Because no one is perfect. An inflated ego stands in the way of an honest evaluation just as does low self-esteem. It doesn't allow a person to see that an asset may have a downside. For example, while you may enjoy a six-figure income, earning it may not leave much time for an intimate relationship. If that's the case, when you meet someone special, you can communicate that flaw up front and find ways to handle it. But without recognizing how one's qualities or circumstances are relative, you're not leaving room for a partner to be open. In other words, a big ego is a wall that can diminish intimacy.

All this introspection doesn't mean you need years in analysis discovering the origins of all your fears, sorting out your relationship with your mother, or positively reinforcing yourself into a healthier lifestyle. You don't have time for that. You want a date for next Saturday.

When you honestly inventory your qualities and examine their pluses and minuses, however, you can become more open and realistic about your needs. This process will enable you to overcome and anticipate objections, and it can help you be more accepting of others— good qualities for a healthy relationship.

As you saw in Chapter 2, Carl minimized his positive qualities by suggesting the opposite qualities in parentheses. The strategy was not only charming, it made him seem more approachable and honest.

The moral? Honesty sells. Strive to communicate that you're a real person. A unique blend of insecurities and ambitions. You'll be more interesting to others—and even if you never place an ad, you'll cultivate deeper relationships.

Some readers may figure they'll avoid the self-examination by embellishing a few facts, sweeping the bad stuff under the rug, and inflating the good stuff. After all, this is advertising. But before you think about creating an ad that knocks five years off your age and 20 pounds off your weight, you should know that every product—from Pepsi to Porsche—is subject to laws and ethical advertising practices that forbid lying and misrepresentation.

Besides, if you truly value yourself, there's no reason to lie about your qualities anyway. In *The Real Rules,* Barbara DeAngelis writes, "When you truly love and respect yourself, you don't have to hide parts of your personality . . . . Masquerade is the opposite of true self-esteem."

Dishonesty slows the process and wastes everyone's time. Ellen, a teacher living in the suburbs of Chicago and an avid personal-ads user, knows this well. She began using the personals to meet people because she disliked contending with the cigarette smoke in bars and didn't dance. Her ad:

> Hoping to meet a beautiful, young, wealthy, voluptuous but thin "girl of his dreams," he anxiously dials five digits from a *Reader* matches ad. Having been disappointed before, he boldly asks, "What do you look like? Are you fat?" "Did I ask if you're bald or wear dentures?" she sarcastically replies. OK, I'm not the girl of your dreams and you're not my knightmare. We're just two non-smokers, S/D, straight (no drugs) WJ persons, between 38–50 yrs or so; who have never been incarcerated or reborn; hanging around the city/burbs together. I'm a female with summers off and you're a male who likes cats, kids, dogs, and pigs.

Not being a beauty queen herself, Ellen liked to think she could see beyond the superficial qualities and was willing to give a guy a chance. However, she found that the men who responded to her ads would lie—a lot.

Sometimes it was not an outright lie; rather, it was that her expectations were dashed because the respondent hadn't been totally up front, which caught her off guard. And that was a turn-off. For example,

Ross, who showed up for a coffee date, hadn't mentioned that he had a chronic skin disease. And Barry had said he was a furniture store owner, five-foot-six-inches, 55 years old, brown hair, and trim. However, when Ellen arrived for their date at the zoo, she found Humpty Dumpty on Geritol. Barry was at least 70 years old, with a balding head and pot-belly. While Ellen has not been discouraged—she does plan on placing more ads—she thinks that a little honesty would be refreshing.

Ellen's experience is not unique. We found both men and women, advertisers and respondents, who were discouraged by the amount of misleading information and downright lies they encountered. Why the lies? When it comes to appearance, some people think that when—or if—they meet, the good may outweigh the bad. Other people just figure that all's fair in love and war. But what does it accomplish? Nothing. Both parties just waste their time and emotional energy.

Does that mean your ad should state that you're as out of shape as a beanbag chair in the basement? That you're unemployed? Bald? Not exactly. You just need to recognize those qualities, so you can communicate truthfully. And there are ways to state almost any fact and have some people find it appealing. You'll learn how to do that in Chapter 6.

Also do keep in mind that readers tend to magnify the importance of the words in an ad. Since they have so little information in which to construct an image, more emphasis is placed on the facts that are stated. Many personal-ad users reported that if they stated that they were, for example, a model or extremely successful, the respondents often had inflated expectations. But if they downplayed their good features, their dates were pleasantly surprised.

Here's Lookin' at Me, Kid

Now that you're ready to look at yourself realistically, you can begin to jot down words and phrases that describe you. But where should you start? Simple—at the beginning and without hesitation. Just get a sheet of paper, or maybe a whole pad, and start writing. This keeps you from editing your thoughts. So here are some inventory strategies. Do each of them quickly. Your first impressions are usually more accurate.

Brainstorm

To create an ad, many copywriters and art directors often begin with a brainstorming session, which is simply putting your thoughts—any thoughts—down on paper. Focus on qualities that describe you. Don't judge. It doesn't matter if your thoughts are silly, arrogant, unflattering, insulting, or bragging. Just spend about 20 minutes writing down whatever adjectives come to mind. They don't even have to be true. You can figure out which ones are true later.

The important thing is to keep the thoughts flowing. Don't pick up your pen from the paper. And don't stop with the adjectives. Write down whatever thoughts you have about yourself. Don't limit your thoughts to the subject of dating either. Any characteristics you note are important. If you think you're repeating yourself, that's OK, too. You'll find this to be a fun exercise, because there's absolutely no way you can mess up. There's absolutely no wrong answer.

Shop the Word Catalogs

Simply stated, creativity is just output from the brain. If there's no input, your output will be limited. So what do you do when you want ideas for a gift or for redecorating a room? You get input by browsing through catalogs or magazines. You window-shop. And you look at the styles in friends' apartments.

To maximize your output in writing your ad, you should do the same. And you don't even have to go far to do it. Just pick up a dictionary, thesaurus, or other word-list book and browse through the words just as you'd do with your favorite department store catalog. Choose as many words as you like—right off the rack, there's no cost—and add them to the list you've created through brainstorming.

When you're tired of looking at *M* words, take the escalator down to the *B* department. Wander around there for a while. Let the words lead you to other words. As before, just keep writing. Concentrate on you. Stop when you have acquired at least 50 words on your word-shopping spree. Don't worry about duplication. Words are free and you can have as many as you like. Overwhelmed by books? Then simply refer to Appendix A for a condensed list of ready-to-use words.

Assess Yourself, Categorically Speaking

Nearly every aspect of compatibility relates to one of the following categories: appearance, activities and recreation, career and abilities, character, community, home life, goals, health, personality, sex, and spirituality. By looking at yourself in terms of each category, you can gain a sense of the parts that make up the whole picture and give yourself a better understanding of who you are. So take out 11 fresh sheets of paper, one for each category, and let the following questions help you draw a picture of yourself. Consider each question mentioned in each category and think of some questions of your own. Remember to use a new sheet or paper for every category even if the previous sheet is not filled with descriptors. And, above all, have fun!

Appearance. This includes not only what you look like, but the other qualities of the senses as well. What color is your hair? Your eyes? Are you tall? Short? Be specific about feet and inches. Are you African American? White? Latino? Native American? Asian? Mixed? How much do you weigh? How old are you? Do you look your age? If not, what age do you look and how do you know? These are standard elements found in most personal ads, so don't stop there. After all, you don't want your ad to sound like everyone else's.

To communicate your uniqueness, elaborate on your features. Start at the top and go for the details. How is your hair styled? Do you have a beard or a mustache? Is anything pierced? Are your lips wide? Do you have a big nose? Perfect teeth? Freckles? Is your hair bushy? Thinning? Are you built like a football player? Is your skin porcelain-like? Is there a style of dress or type of clothing you prefer? How are your eyes shaped? Do you have a wandering eye? Do you usually look serious? Playful? Seductive?

How would you describe your physical style? Are you rugged? Sexy? Studious? Prudish? Sophisticated? Casual? Country? Graceful? Professional? Plodding?

Move down your body. How is it shaped? Do you have broad shoulders? Are you hairy? Do you have a tiny waist? Large breasts? Muscular arms? Tattoos? Thin legs? Big feet? Short legs? Paunch? Tight butt? Secretary spread? Are you bowlegged? Do you have any physical disabilities? Are you missing a finger? Hand? Leg?

Is there a particular scent you like to wear? Do you look like someone famous? Are you a combination of famous faces or personalities? Is there someone famous you identify with? What do you sound like? Do you have a deep voice? Raspy? Whiny? Do you laugh a lot? Cry a lot? Snort? Burp? Squeak? Remember, write it all down, the good and the bad.

Activities and Recreational Interests. How do you spend your free time? How much free time do you have? Do you prefer group activities or are you a loner? Do you like bowling? Theater? Do you have hobbies? Collections? Do you like sports? Which ones? As a spectator or a participant? Do you like cultural activities? What sort? Who are your favorite musical artists? Are you artistic? In what way? Do you like to travel? Long or short trips? To where? How do you like to get there? What do you like to do once you get there? Do you like to read? Books or magazines? On what subject? Do you prefer to be outdoors or indoors? Are you a night person or do you prefer rising early? What do you like to do to unwind? Do you take classes?

Career and Abilities. These factors greatly affect relationships. What do you do for a living? Is your job a large part of your life? Does it require a college education? A partner of equal status? Does your job require travel? If so, how much? How dedicated are you? Is your job a job or a lifestyle? Do you work overtime? Do you have an erratic schedule? Is your job dangerous? How much money do you make? Do you squirrel money away or live for today? Are you famous—or do you hope to be? Is your career low-paying but meaningful? Do you work with confidential information? Do you like to talk about your work outside of the office? Are you in debt? Philanthropic? Creative? Intelligent? Educated? Do you like owning things? Do you have a special talent?

Character. This is one of the most important aspects of a relationship because it helps overcome differences in other categories. It's a gauge of maturity, and of ability to commit and handle responsibility. How honest are you with yourself? With others? Are you courageous? Can you stand up for yourself and others? How loyal are you? How fair?

Flexible? Willing to learn and grow? What are your values? Do you practice what you preach?

Your Community. Are you involved in it? Do you live in the city? Suburbs? A rural area? Do you like your neighbors? Do you have a lot of friends and acquaintances? Are you involved in politics? Do you support a political party? Are you involved in your church? School system? How much time do you devote to community activities each month? How do you relate to other races or nationalities? How important is it that your partner shares the same interests and attitudes?

Home Life. Describe it. Where were you born? Do your parents live near you? Do you like your mother? Father? How big a family do you have? What nationality are you? To what extent does your nationality affect the way you live? Are you a twin? How big is your household? Do you have pets? Do you want children of your own? Are you divorced? Are you on friendly terms with your ex? Do you already have children? How many? How old? Are you the custodial parent? If not, how often do you see your children? Do you want more children? Do you enjoy celebrating holidays with your family? Taking vacations with family? Do you care for any disabled/aging family members? What kind of baggage are you dealing with?

Goals. What are they? When you consider all the other categories, what would you like to change about where you stand in them? Do you want to change jobs? Why? Do you want to move? To where? Why? What's your idea of success? What are you doing to reach these goals? Where do you see yourself next year? In five years? Ten years? Fifteen years?

This is also the place to include everything you learned in Chapter 2. What kind of relationship do you want? Do you want children of your own? What's your time frame? Don't only think about your goals in terms of a romantic relationship. This is about you as an individual and your life.

Your Health. How do you describe it? What do you do to stay healthy? Do you have any disabilities? Chronic illnesses? If you want children, are you able to have them? Do you have a lot of physical energy? Mental energy? Do you work out regularly? Do you participate in sports? Are you a vegetarian? Do you favor an alternative or traditional approach to medicine? Do you have any illnesses that are hereditary? How do you handle stress? Do you have an addiction? What have you done to control it? Have you ever been in therapy? What did you learn?

Personality. This counts—especially in your relationships. How do you describe your personality and character? Outgoing? Introverted? Serious? Are you always late or always early? Moody? Energetic? Sarcastic? Humorous? Unconventional? Conservative? Liberal? Radical? Rebellious? Needy? Bitter? Optimistic? Intelligent? In what ways do you take risks and in what ways do you require security? Do you have a short fuse? An easygoing attitude? Are you forgiving or do you hold grudges? Are you generous? Adventurous? Insecure? What is your astrological sign? Do you believe it makes a difference? What are your fears? What makes you feel proud?

Sex. Of course, your interest, or lack of interest, in sex is a large part of any romantic relationship. Do you consider yourself inhibited or uninhibited? Passionate? Are you heterosexual, bisexual, or homosexual? If bisexual or homosexual, are you out of the closet? How often do you want to have sex? Is duration important to you? Are there particular sexual activities you enjoy? Do you have any fetishes? Do you watch X-rated videos? Are you into nontraditional forms of sexual play? Nudism? Voyeurism? Swapping partners? Being dominant or submissive?

Spirituality. How do you feel about it? What determines your moral and ethical code of behavior? Do you follow an established religion? Are you involved with your church or temple? Do want to date only someone from your faith? Do you believe in waiting for marriage before having sex? Does your religion have rules against marrying someone who is divorced? Do you want to raise your children in a particular faith? Are you willing to marry someone who has a different faith than yours? Do you believe in life after death? Is it important that your partner believe as you do?

Did we miss anything? Surely. These questions were designed to get you going. Just keep writing down your thoughts in the appropriate categories.

Compare Yourself to Others

Another method of identifying your characteristics is to compare yourself to others. Take a piece of paper and write down the major traits you constantly encounter in others that are very different or similar to your own. Think about coworkers, family members, and friends.

What do you have in common with them? How are you different from them? In what ways do you wish you were more like them? Less like them? In what ways do you excel? What habits of theirs most annoy you? What does that say about you?

Additionally, who are your heroes? Whom do you admire? A hero can be a famous sports figure, movie star, historical figure, or your grandfather. What causes you to feel admiration? What does this say about you? Do your heroes represent qualities you want to have or qualities you want in those around you?

Ask Other People

How do your family and friends describe you? Ask them and you may be surprised at their responses. What qualities do they think a partner would find most appealing in you? Most unappealing? What annoying habits do you have? In past relationships, how did your partners describe you?

If you're afraid you won't get honest answers, share your thoughts about your faults. If you acknowledge them first, people may be more comfortable being honest with you. Write down their comments on a fresh sheet of paper, whether you agree with them or not. Then wait a few days before reading over the comments and cross out any you think are inaccurate. Don't just eliminate the negative comments. Give each item careful consideration and save only the ones that you really feel are true.

Another way to get an honest answer might be to try therapy. Sometimes after an unhappy marriage or a series of bad relationships, it's a good idea to invest in a little therapy to see if you're choosing the wrong partners due to an inaccurate perception of yourself or a lack of awareness of your true needs.

If you've already seen a therapist, think about what you learned about yourself—your needs, habits, and challenges. These are all valid items for your inventory. Write them down on a separate piece of paper.

Get a Charge Out of Your Positive and Negative Qualities

Focusing on oneself isn't usually a comfortable endeavor. If you let the negative traits you've uncovered dominate your self-perception, they can make you feel unlovable. This is a good time to sit back and give yourself a break. You're no better or worse at being a loving partner than anyone else. And there are plenty of people who have negative traits who enjoy very rewarding relationships.

The trick is to understand that your negative and positive traits have trade-offs. Jeff described himself as a "complete leper in the dating world"—a single parent, short, religious—everything that's not hip or cool. You can see his self-perception clearly in his ad:

> DWM, 27, 5'4" born-again, down-to-earth, custodial dad of one son, seeks S/DWF 22 to 30 for possible relationship.

Being a custodial parent means Jeff's probably better able to handle responsibility and understand women who are in similar circumstances. His spiritual life is also appealing to a person with similar values. And to a woman who is five-foot-two, Jeff's height is just fine. But Jeff's ad lacked an upbeat attitude—one that reflects the pride he should feel. He did receive four responses, but so far nothing has clicked.

Like Jeff, nearly every quality you've inventoried has both a positive and a negative side. Once you understand this, acknowledging the qualities you would like to change is less threatening. If a divorce or other circumstance makes you feel like a failure, understand that your past has given you insights that you wouldn't otherwise have. On the

other hand, if you're proud that you've achieved a demanding, rewarding career, understand that the energy required to maintain it can make
your personal life suffer. On a more subtle level, ask yourself if your
easygoing nature is a sign of insecurity and a need to be accepted.

Trish learned this, too. A therapist, she was married for nine and
a half years before her husband died. She lacked confidence. Who'd
want a widow, she wondered. But she decided to try the personals
anyway. Here's her ad:

> Rosie O'Donnell seeks Drew Carey. Big, beautiful, bubbly. SWF,
> 42 N/S, N/D, enjoys slow dancing, spectator sports, comedy, quiet
> dinners. Seeking respectful, romantic, stable WM, 35–45 N/S,
> big/tall preferred.

She regarded her personality and build as similar to Rosie O'Donnell's,
so she thought the comparison was an accurate one and put a positive
spin on the facts. "I'm not going to apologize for how much room I take
up on this planet," she said with a laugh. She may not be a beauty
queen, but she communicated confidence. And she didn't explain that
she was a widow because she felt it misrepresented her state of mind.
She was done grieving and was eager to get on with living.

"I'm only 42 and when people hear I'm a widow, it freaks 'em
out," she said.

She received about 20 responses, most of which were in her age
range. She suspected that about five of them were from married or
attached men because they didn't leave a home number. Some said
they were in the midst of moving and others only left a pager number.

Another five responses came from men who seemed nice, but she
didn't know why they responded because they had nothing in common with her. Another five responses were from men who were worth
meeting. One was a widower, but she sensed that he was still mourn-
ing his wife's death.

Another she met for coffee. Their meeting ended up lasting for
six hours.

"We just clicked," she said. "Two minutes into the conversation we connected on every major issue. There was a genuine person-to-person connection."

Placing the ad made her realize that there were men out there who were interested in her for who she was. The experience built up her confidence and helped her recognize that there are men out there worth meeting. In fact, after this experience she started planning to approach an acquaintance in her office building about going to lunch sometime.

Like Trish, accept yourself. And expect that others will accept you. You'll also learn to accept others. This is an attitude adjustment that opens the door to many wonderful possibilities.

You might even be having doubts about yourself: "I'm overweight." "Bald." "I'm too short/too tall." "I've got herpes/a low-paying job/no education/small children/roommates."

Those are critical voices—yours and others'—that can drown out self-esteem and keep your life on hold. People listen to those voices all the time and use all sorts of excuses to avoid pursuing a partner. Remember Bob from earlier in this chapter? He let all sorts of voices hold him back. And the more critical you are with yourself, the more critical you are likely to be with others, which lessens your chances for a healthy relationship.

That doesn't mean everyone is "marketable." Some people have problems that would be unfair to impose on a partner. Serious problems, such as addictions, legal issues, and out-of-control psychiatric disorders should be resolved before placing an ad. This can involve a 12-step program, counseling, medical care, or legal help. A potential partner should know what to expect and what you're doing to improve your situation.

Accept That You Can't Appeal to Everyone

No matter how hard Chrysler may try to appeal to a younger market, it will never win over the majority of people likely to purchase a Camaro. However, that fact in no way diminishes Chrysler's ability to be a truly successful corporation.

And just as Chrysler's product managers may try to make their product lines faster or sleeker, many of us imagine that we will be satisfied with ourselves when we are richer or thinner. While these may be worthwhile pursuits, to have a satisfying relationship you must first be satisfied with yourself. If you don't fully accept the fact that no matter how rich, attractive, and successful you are, you will not appeal to everyone, then you're not looking at yourself realistically. A lack of realism will hamper your ability to recognize your strengths and weaknesses—which is critical in successful marketing.

Realize You Only Need to Attract One Person

Unless you want to build your little black book into a volume collection, you really don't have to be concerned that your appearance or bank account is less than ideal. You'll be surprised by how many people will find you attractive. No one characteristic dictates this. We are the sum total of all our qualities.

Change Yourself (Or Don't)

Crash diets. Nose jobs. A new career. These are other ways you can deal with your negative attributes. But while improving yourself can open the door to more possibilities in your relationships, such changes may not always be right for you.

Let's say you're the marketing genius in a national food corporation and your focus-group research shows that people prefer a creamier, richer apple pie than the latest recipe the company cooks have concocted. You have two options. You can change your recipe to appeal to the tastes of the masses. Or you can turn the negatives into positives. For example, a less rich, less creamy apple pie probably has fewer calories and less fat. Maybe you can sell this pie as a healthier alternative to your competitor's product. Your message should focus on the pie's advantages. Just like the marketing executive, you need to decide:

- Is this trait changeable?
- Do you *want* to change it?
- Is it worth changing?

If you answered no to any of these questions, then you'd probably be better off not trying to change the trait. Then you'd need to devise a strategy to deal with it. This is the challenge of the marketing process: turning negatives into positives.

Narrow It Down to the Critical Few

If you've done the previous exercises, you're probably thinking, "Gee, I've got pages of scribbles that describe myself, but what does all this have to do with writing a personal ad?" The answer? Everything! If you're seeking a serious relationship, or even a rewarding friendship, these are qualities you'd like to know about another person; therefore you can assume these are things someone else will want to know about you.

But there's so much material here. So now you just need to boil it down to a message that communicates who you are. Remember the 11 categories? Take the pages you created—appearance; activities and recreational interests; career and abilities; character; community; home life; goals; health; personality; sex; and spirituality—and incorporate the traits from the other methods into the appropriate categories. For example, your brainstorming list may have included that you love eating out. Add that fact to the recreational activities list. Did therapy teach you that you need a lot of affection from a partner? Note that in the sex category. Circle recurring items or themes. These are of special importance to your ad.

Once you have each of your items in one of the 11 categories, you need to condense the information. first eliminate duplications. Cross out words that are similar to other words—except if they have nuances that make them mean something slightly different, in which case leave them. For example, *affectionate* and *sensuous* are similar, but have different connotations; whereas using both *faithful* and *loyal* may be redundant.

Next, on each page, circle the 10 words or phrases that are most important to you—whether good or bad. Your appearance category might include a great figure or you may take pride in your shocking red hair. On the other hand, you may feel horribly insecure about your teeth or weight. Circle the 10 qualities in each category that affect you the most. Then, put a star next to the items that you feel are *most* important for your partner to know about you.

Put aside these pages and save them for Chapter 6, because now you need to decide the qualities of the person you want, which will be another important portion of your ad's content.

Cupid Shoots
for a Star

Nothing's beautiful from every point of view.

—Horace

We're all familiar with those old Hollywood movies, where the boy and girl come from different worlds, they don't get along, they fight, they kiss and break up, but in the end they fall in love and live happily ever after. Just one question: What happened *after* the happily ever after? True, if all you want is an anonymous interlude, then compatibility with your partner isn't that important. But if you want to share your life with someone, we're sure you'll agree, it becomes critical. Relationships are difficult enough without constantly having to compromise on everything. If you prefer to spend your shared income on a three-week African safari while your spouse wants a big-screen TV—you've got a problem. Or if you're a stay-at-home couch potato and you fall madly in love with a party animal, you can expect that this conflict will create friction in your relationship.

Luckily, with the personals, you have a unique opportunity to screen out people who are not compatible with you. And it's easy to do. So take advantage of it. Once you've figured out the attributes you want to communicate about yourself, just take the next critical step and think about the qualities of the person you want to attract. This will help you identify your target audience.

Tony turned to the personals for just that reason. Not only was he interested in a New Age lifestyle, he was shy and felt that it was easier to approach a relationship through the ads. "Our society is so fearful," he said. "It's difficult to get to know people." There were a few women in his building that he would have liked to get to know, but they didn't even return his hello when he saw them. So with the encouragement of a friend who'd met his girlfriend through the personals, he decided to try them himself.

At first he just responded to ads, but since none of the women he called returned his voice-mail messages, he thought he'd place one of his own. His first ad (not shown) attracted seven responses. He met five of the women and began to see one of them steadily until she realized she was still emotionally tied to her former lover. Two of the other messages he didn't return because of the sound of their voices. Tony said that he felt shallow for letting their voices sway him—but he also said he preferred not to explore a relationship with them when he felt strongly that he would be backing out later.

The following ad is his second attempt.

> In Recovery from Western Civilization: 44, DWM, into body training, values any path with heart, hangs out with Buddha, Neem Karoli Baba, Christ, and others, learning from our first teachers: the Earth and her children; macrobiotic (but not neurotic about it); two teenage sons (who live with mom); values balance and caring over statistics and ego; ns; Chicago. You: yourself living your healing journey, want to share it with another.

As you can see, this home health nurse and former engineer isn't likely to find the woman of his dreams at the local night spot. So far Tony's ad received six responses; all of whom expressed a desire for more contact with nature and spirituality. Again two of the woman had no appeal. But he's had promising conversations with two others.

Tony also passed up a message left by a woman with a harsh, rough voice. "I hate to admit it," he said, "but I just couldn't listen to that every day for the rest of my life." He also didn't call a woman who emphasized her ability to remain faithful and monogamous. She said she wanted to marry. Tony felt she wanted to have more than a husband. She sounded too emotionally needy.

As you can see, Tony had a strong idea of the characteristics of the women he wanted to reach. It helped him eliminate respondents from contention and it also helped him set the tone of his ad and to clarify what he wanted from his dream partner.

To communicate effectively, you need to know who you're trying to reach. To do this in consumer advertising, marketers study demographics and other information—age, ethnic group, location, and other factors (which you'll learn more about in the next chapter)—to find the people most likely to use the product. The need to identify the target is even more apparent in recruitment advertising that you'll find in the help-wanted section of your newspaper. Here, an employer will describe the position, the company, advancement potential, and the benefits. In addition, a good recruitment ad states the job requirements, including educational level, experience, need for transportation, and necessary skills. Stating these necessary requirements saves both readers and employers a lot of time. While some people may apply randomly to any job, a smart job search would only spend time on those positions that look like a match.

When you know the type of person you want to reach, personal ads offer a strong advantage over other avenues of meeting people because you can target exactly the kind of person that interests you. Having a clear idea of the kind of person you want also helps you choose *where* to place your ad.

What happens when you're not specific? Let's look at Lori's experience. Giving, sane, attractive, and creative, she was in her early 40s and had never been married. Her problem was that she wanted a long-term relationship with two different types of men in the same body: one an irreverent, adventurous, artistic, complex bad-boy; the other a financially successful, attractive, and health-conscious professional. To find this man, Lori placed the following ad on-line and got 19 responses:

Men, Take a Chance
Seeking to meet a SWM 35–45 who is passionate, great sense
of humor, likes to get out and do things (the usual stuff) and yet
have a great laid-back evening at home, honest, down-to-earth,
has a job. Any religion OK. I'm a SWJF, 42, people say I look
about 34, dark brown hair, big brown eyes, 5'5", medium build,
work out 3–4 times a week (don't let that scare you), I'm a free-
lance designer, I paint when I can, read, go to movies, dine out,
enjoy watching sports, straightforward, good heart, etc. If you
want to know more about me, e-mail.

As you can see, Lori did a good job of communicating what she likes
to do, but not the qualities she wanted. So she received responses from
many different kinds of men. Ben was a divorced sales manager with
two children. Greg, divorced with one son, was a chief engineer.
Bruno was an Atlanta-based pilot with a major commercial airline who
regularly traveled to Lori's city. Chuck, never married, was an energetic real estate developer. Bryan was a divorced dad and worked for a
construction company.

Although Lori corresponded with several of the men for several
weeks and even arranged to meet a few, she didn't form a relationship
with any of them. Maybe if Lori had been more specific about the
qualities she wanted, she would have had a stronger basis on which
to form a relationship. At the very least, they would have had interests
in common.

Like Lori, Shawn didn't get very descriptive either. A 36-year-old
divorced sales representative and father of three, Shawn didn't have any
trouble meeting women in bars, airplanes, restaurants—or wherever else
he went, for that matter. He even had romances with some of the
women he met in these places, but he found that "most [of them] just
wanted to have fun." But after two and a half years of the single life,
Shawn was more interested in forming a long-term relationship.

To acquaint himself with the personal-ads culture, Shawn listened
to dozens of voice-mail ads before leaving a message. He first advertised
in *The Village Voice,* but didn't receive a single response. Then, figuring

that meeting women on-line would give him an opportunity to get to know them a little better, he placed the following ad on a computer bulletin board.

> ISO S/DWF, 28–36, of healthy mind and body. Busy schedules, happy lives, desires romance, shared experiences. Take a chance, I may be the one, you may be too!

His approach was to be positive, sincere, and sane. But what did his ad really say? What constituted a healthy mind and body? And he said he had a "busy schedule," but doing what? Plus, he said he was "happy," but what about his life made him that way? What sorts of experiences did he look forward to sharing? Being more specific would have told readers more about him, the kind of person he wanted to meet, and what kind of relationship he wanted to share. But even with his vague ad, Shawn received responses. He spoke with several of the women on the phone and arranged to meet a few of them in restaurants.

Some, he said, were very nice women—and some were attractive. Most were divorced women with children. Melinda responded with the comment, "Don't be shy," which prompted him to invite her out to talk. He then met Sarah, who described herself as Cher, while he discovered she was more like "a short version of Tiny Tim." And she scared him away by bringing sex into the conversation during their first meeting. Debbie was attractive; unfortunately there was no chemistry between them. Gretchen was warm, attractive, and intelligent, but she reminded him of his sister.

So who did Shawn really want? "The one that got away," he said. Soon after he was divorced, friends arranged a blind date for him with a newly divorced woman. Mary was sweet, educated, family-oriented, and giving. They became involved and fell in love. But it soon became apparent that Mary wanted a family of her own—something that Shawn had already accomplished and wasn't interested in doing again.

They soon realized they were each other's "transitional person" and they went their separate ways. Maybe if Shawn were to rewrite his ad describing Mary's best qualities, one of his respondents would be the woman for him.

From these stories, you can see that it's important to decide on what qualities are important to you. Managers of dating services have complained to us that their clients leaf through books or sit through reels of eligible single people and insist they don't see "it." Their ideal. The *one* for them. The person with all of their must-haves.

Being a nonsmoker or nondrinker is a common requirement. When people are looking for marriage, they may want a person of the same religion—and someone who is willing and able to raise a family. And, of course, both sexes seek the ambiguous quality of attractiveness.

That doesn't seem like too much to ask for. Then why is it so difficult for people to find someone? It's not. Wonderful potential partners are right under their noses. If you've done a good job of figuring out who you are and communicating the kind of person you want for a partner, you'll be more likely to meet someone with whom you can click.

So what makes for compatibility? In *Are You the One for Me?*, Barbara DeAngelis offers a 60-second checklist of questions you should ask yourself:

- Would you want to have a child with this person?
- Would you want to have a child just like this person?
- Do you want to become more like this person?
- Would you be willing to spend your life with this person if he or she never changed?

If you can answer yes to these four questions, you're on your way to finding a compatible relationship.

Here's Looking at You, Kid

Of course, to identify the traits that make up the four questions listed above takes more work. So where should you start? Just follow the process described in the rest of this chapter. It's much like the work you did in Chapter 3, except this time, instead of focusing on yourself, you're concentrating on the partner of your dreams. Let's start now. Get out some more paper and start writing. As in the last chapter, do each exercise quickly, because your first impressions are usually pretty accurate.

Brainstorm

Just as you did in the previous chapter, spend about 20 minutes jotting down whatever adjectives or phrases come to mind about your ideal partner. They don't even have to be realistic. Just keep going. And don't stop with adjectives or phrases. Write down every thought you have, whatever comes to mind. Any characteristics you note are important. If you repeat yourself, that's OK. You might find something interesting in the repetition. Just keep your thoughts flowing. Don't pick up your pen from the paper. There's no right or wrong here. If you find anything you don't want, you can edit it out—later, after the exercise has been completed.

Shop the Word Catalogs Again

Browse through the dictionary or thesaurus just as you did in the last chapter. Let the words lead you to other words or spark images. Keep writing, concentrating on what you want in your ideal partner.

If you find any characteristic you don't want, just edit it out after you've completed the exercise. But before you erase it, ask yourself, "Why did I write it down in the first place? What does that really say about the person I want to meet?" This will help you dig deeper into finding the characteristics in a partner.

Can't think of any words or don't have a dictionary handy? Then use our list of adjectives in Appendix A. Just go down each column until you find the right words. Stop when you have about 50 words.

Then refer to the list you created in Chapter 3 that describes you. How many of those words also describe the qualities you want in a partner? There should be many. Copy down those words as well. This will ensure that your partner is compatible with you in many areas of your life.

Return to the Categories

If you address each of the qualities you went through in Chapter 3, you'll cover the gamut in describing your ideal partner. So take out 11 clean sheets of paper, and have one category per page. Carefully go through each category, answering the questions we ask; then think up other questions that we may not have asked and answer them as well.

Appearance. As in Chapter 3, we'll begin here. Sometimes advertisers ask for movie-star look-alikes. Doing this can be an efficient and creative way to state many qualities with one concept. But while this approach can help you identify your dream person, it has a few drawbacks, because it focuses too much attention on appearance. The reference to a movie star may catch readers' eyes and make respondents feel that they have an edge. However, they often disregard the other qualities that are important. If you've asked for a clone of Ginger from *Gilligan's Island,* your collection of respondents could resemble a casting call for a reunion episode. That doesn't sound too bad, but you might waste a lot of time sorting out the smokers from the nonsmokers, the honest from the dishonest, the mothers from the childless women, as well as many other categories of attributes that you may care about.

How do you get around this drawback? Simple: If you've had a crush on Meg Ryan for years and can't resist trying to attract a reasonable facsimile, then end your ad with "Meg Ryan look-alike a plus." Then your statement is not of a must-have quality; rather, you have simply identified a type of appearance that would interest you. Then your ad can include not only your ideal for the appearance of your partner, but other qualities as well.

So ask yourself: does hair color matter? Weight? Height? Age? Be specific. What weight? What height? What age? Again, these are standard elements to most personal ads, so don't stop there. Elaborate with details. Do you like a beard or a mustache? Piercings? Wide lips? Perfect teeth? Freckles? Stocky or lean build? Is there a style of dress or a type of clothing that you prefer? Do you mind eyeglasses? Baldness? Do you like broad shoulders? Lots of hair? Do you like to see a tiny waist? Large breasts? Muscular arms? Tattoos? Thin legs? Long legs? Tight butt? Write it all down.

What about personal style? Do you want a rugged man or the three-piece-suit type? A sexy vamp or the girl next door? Studious? Sophisticated? Casual? Country? Graceful? Professional?

Is there a particular scent you like? Is your ideal partner a combination of famous faces or personalities? Are you sensitive about the type of voice a person has? The type of laugh? Think about people you find extremely attractive. What is it about them that attracts you? You may find there are qualities that have less to do with appearance and more to do with confidence and style.

Interests and Recreational Activities. You've already listed what you like to do in the exercises in Chapter 3, but is it important that your partner spend a lot of time with you? Or do you prefer a more independent person? Do you want your partner to join you in group activities like bridge or bowling? Do you like to go with a partner to the theater? Do you want to share hobbies? Do you want someone who enjoys the same sports as you do? Which ones? As a spectator or as a participant? Are cultural activities part of the picture with a partner? Do you need someone who shares your musical tastes? Do you want him or her to travel with you? On long or short trips? To where? Are there magazines whose readership represents the type of person you want to know? Do you have strange hours and want your partner to keep strange hours too?

Careers and Abilities. Consider the type of occupation you want in a mate. Do you want someone who is financially independent? Is it important if he or she makes more, or less, money than you do? Why? Is it important for your partner to hold an advanced degree? Why?

Character. This is one of the most important aspects of a person. Why? Because character is a gauge of maturity. It indicates an ability to commit and handle responsibility. It will help you handle tough times. When partners are incompatible in other ways, good character traits will help ease the conflicts those differences create. In her book *Are You the One for Me?*, Barbara DeAngelis recommends that you look for six character traits in a mate: commitment to personal growth (willingness to change); emotional openness; integrity; maturity and responsibility; high self-esteem; and a positive attitude toward life.

Community. From what type of community do you want to choose a partner? An urban setting? Suburban? Rural? Why? Do you want a partner who has many friends and/or one who shares your friends? Do you want a mate who is close with his or her family? Do you like to spend holidays with relatives? Is it important that your partner be able to relate to many other races or nationalities, or that he or she be of a particular nationality? Are there political or religious groups you find intolerable? Why?

Home Life. Describe the home life of your ideal partner. What if he or she lives with parents? Children? Is it important that your partner not come from a broken home? Do you prefer someone from a big family? What about pets? Are you open to someone who is divorced? Recently divorced? Separated? Or do want someone who has never married? What about children? Is it important that your partner be free of a demanding ex-wife or -husband? Small children? Disabled and/or aging family members? What kind of baggage are you willing—or unwilling—to accommodate?

Goals. What goals should this person have? Early retirement? Retirement with you to Arizona or Florida? Retirement with you to a foreign country? Long road trips? World travel? Should he or she want to work up the corporate ladder? Become famous? Save a million bucks? Save the world (or at least a small part of it)? Experience many different occupations or hobbies? Win a trivia contest? You name it. And perhaps you can find it (or, more accurately, him or her).

Health. How important is your partner's health? Do you want someone to join you in challenging physical activities? Do you want a vegetarian? A meat-and-potatoes person? Someone who is energetic? Will you date someone who drinks alcohol? Or abstains from any drinking? Smokes pot? Does drugs? Or abstains completely? Do you want someone who is nutrition conscious or someone who is willing to use a drive-through for meals?

Personality. Of course, this counts a lot. What traits are compatible with yours? Outgoing? Introverted? Energetic? Affectionate? Confident? Curious? Open-minded? Serious? Outspoken? Optimistic? Dependable? Sarcastic? Humorous? Unconventional? Conservative? Liberal? Radical? Rebellious? Intelligent? A risk-taker? Easygoing? Forgiving? Generous? Adventurous? Insecure?

And there are more questions you may ask to get a more specific picture: How important are courage, honesty, integrity, and determination in a partner? How independent must he or she be? Does he or she need to be able to function alone for long periods of time? Is it important to be debt-free? To balance your checkbook? To plan for retirement? Or to be generous? Philanthropic? Creative? Intelligent? What astrological sign is he or she compatible with? (Hey, why not take it into consideration? Many potential mates do!)

Sex. Do you want a partner who is experimental? Uninhibited? Passionate? Modest? Bisexual? Straight? Gay? If bisexual or gay, do you want a partner who is out of the closet? How often do you want to have sex? Are there particular sexual activities you want your partner to enjoy? Do you want someone to share nontraditional sexual play? Nudism? Voyeurism? Swapping partners? Being dominant or submissive? Do you have any fetishes that you want a partner to satisfy?

Spirituality. How do you feel about spirituality in your partner? How important is it that he or she have a moral or ethical code of behavior? A clean criminal record? Believe in an established religion? Not believe in anything at all? Believe in the same religion as you believe? Do you want your mate to be involved with his or her church or temple? Do you want a partner who'll understand that you want to wait for marriage before having sex?

Compare Your Ideal Partner to Others

Another method of identifying the characteristics of your ideal partner is to compare him or her to other people in your life. It's easy. Just
take a piece of paper and write down all the major traits you constantly encounter in your friends and acquaintances. Think about
coworkers, family members, and friends. What do you want your partner to have in common with them? And how should he or she be different from them?

Who are your heroes or people you admire? A hero can be a
famous movie star, sports figure, historical figure, even your grandfather. You don't even need to let reality stop you. Your hero could be
a fictional character—or even a cartoon one. What causes you to feel
admiration for this person (or character)? How does he or she represent the qualities you want in a mate?

Ask Other People

What sort of person do your family and friends want for you? Ask
them and you may be surprised at their responses. What qualities do
they think best suit you? What qualities did they like or dislike about
people you've dated in the past?

Write down their comments on a fresh sheet of paper, whether you
agree with them or not. Then wait a few days before going back to this
list. Cross out the comments that you think are inaccurate. Give each
item careful consideration and save the ones that you feel are true. Be
careful here. You may discover that you've been looking for someone
to please your parents more than to please yourself. If your parents'
expectations for your mate match the qualities you've already identified, you should question if you're really thinking for yourself. On
the other hand, sometimes as an act of rebellion, people purposely
choose partners who will irritate their parents. If the qualities you've
identified so far are the very opposite of the expectations of your family, question whether you're trying to make a rebellious statement. Letting family and friends direct your choices, either through compliance
or rebellion, is no way to find a healthy relationship. If advice seems
right, use it. If not, ignore it.

Examine Previous Relationships

What qualities did you most admire in people you've dated in the past? Include those on your list. In reviewing this group, you may also discover qualities you want to avoid. It's important to recognize those as well. However, be aware of the natural tendency to focus on compensating for your negative experiences. After dating an alcoholic, you may be so focused on finding a partner who stays sober that other important qualities seem trivial. Maintain an objective perspective. If you've ever been in therapy, you probably learned things about the sort of person who is good for you. So write down what you've learned about your choices. Are you still trying to resolve relationship issues with your mother, father, or even a past partner? These observations are valid items for your list and you should keep them with your other observations.

Narrow It Down to the Critical Few

As you did in Chapter 3, you've once again created pages of scribbles. So how do you choose which characteristics to focus on in your ad? Just use the same strategy you used to inventory your own qualities.

Take all of the pages and incorporate the traits from the other strategies into the appropriate area. Again, circle recurring items or themes. These are of special importance to your ad.

Once you have each of the items in one of the 11 categories, you need to condense the information. first, cross out the duplicates or similar words. If the words have connotations that make them slightly different, leave both on the list.

Next, on each page, circle the 10 words or phrases that you feel are very important in your mate. Appearance might include a great figure, a certain height or other attributes. Then, put a star next to the items that you feel are *most* important in your partner.

This is your list of must-haves. These are items that you find critical, the basics that you'd feel cheated without. They can be as superficial as a full head of hair or as deep as a shared religion, the important thing is that you now have a better idea of who you want. Put aside these pages and save them for Chapter 6. Of course, you'll also decide on the latitude points—attributes you'd like in a mate, but that are not necessary. These will help when you analyze responses, guiding you in prioritizing which person to call back first. So save this list for Chapter 8.

Then Go Back to Reality

OK, you've had your head in the clouds fantasizing about Mr. or Ms. Right. But now it's time to give your list the once-over and see if you're being realistic.

In his book *Finding the Love of Your Life,* Neil Clark Warren states that "unrealistic expectations" are a cause of "faulty mate selection." Many singles walk around with an ideal in their heads and measure potential partners against it. Inevitably, they get very infatuated with a person, but then become quickly disillusioned when he or she falls off the pedestal. That's why it's important to check your list and make sure you're being realistic.

It's also important to consider whether you're likely to find your choice of qualities within one person. Are you looking for someone who is very ambitious, but also willing to spend lazy evenings and weekends relaxing with you? That may be frustrating for an ambitious person. Or you may be stimulated by a date's unpredictable, spontaneous personality but disappointed that he or she is often undependable. Do you want a glamorous woman, but resent the time and money she spends on cosmetics, workouts, and wardrobe?

Don't worry. There's a way to satisfy these diverse needs. Communicate your need for balance between these traits. Simply becoming aware that you have difficult-to-meet expectations helps you become more charitable about judging others. This awareness also helps prevent you from trying to turn a person into someone else.

There are also all kinds of relationships between exact opposites, but those require compromise, and let's face it, life is tough enough without adding more compromise. In *Finding the Love of Your Life,* Neil Clark Warren suggests that you find a partner who is a lot like yourself. He argues that when it comes to values, intelligence, intimacy, interests, and expectations about roles, similarities are essential. Differences in energy level, personal habits, use of money, and verbal skills spell trouble.

With this in mind, Ann, a single mother for 10 years and raising a son, looked for a clone. Here's her short but to-the-point ad, which she had placed with an on-line personal-ad service:

> Self-directed DWF, 52, seeking WM 50–65 who also loves the arts, travel, reading, and computers for ultimately LTR.

This was her first ad, but it at least provided a small hint into her interests, the kind of relationship she was seeking, and the interests she wanted in a mate. She received about 100 responses from a cross section of the population. She corresponded with a number of men via e-mail and, after a few messages, ventured into phone conversations. She made dates to meet five of them.

Meanwhile, Gerry, who'd enjoyed skimming the ads, was living on the West Coast and had been raising two daughters. Divorced for 10 years and with retirement from his job as a school principal just around the corner, he felt he was ready to share his time with a life-long partner.

He responded to four or five ads and became pen pals with a few of them but was seeking a woman who had "a mind of her own"—someone who was a "slightly less than radical feminist." He also wanted someone who shared some of his interests. But to be truly compatible, the woman of his dreams had to be quirky—"a little strange"—because he kept odd hours and many times started his day at 3 A.M. So when he stumbled on Ann's ad, he was impressed with her description of herself as self-directed. He felt that this indicated she had an independent streak, so he left her a message.

Ann and Gerry sent e-mails back and forth twice a day for six weeks. There were intimate conversations. They shared ideas and opinions. Gerry was skeptical, but Ann wasn't. She trusted her intuition. She'd been right about the other men she'd met.

They decided to meet in Las Vegas. And they married there three days later. Ann then returned home and packed her bags and business for the move across the country.

Now, after nearly a year of marriage, Gerry seems surprised at how well they have been getting along. Sure there were adjustments, but Gerry says that deep down, they are so compatible that the pluses far outweigh the minuses.

Liz also wanted to find someone who was compatible, so rather than just describing her interests, she also included the qualities she was seeking. Like Ann she was able to describe herself and the man she wanted to meet within a limited amount of space.

> Beauty—7, humor—9, brains—7, passion—9, secure—6, jealous—2, wackiness—9, athletic—5, adventurous—7, neurotic—5, age—37, mom of 2, DWF, creative professional wants rel. w/DW dad with similar ratings. Just do it!

Liz placed this ad in a popular urban newspaper and received about 16 responses. The majority of respondents also used the rating system to score themselves. She dated five of them. Three of them were very compatible—and very promising. But because of her busy life raising her two children and working full-time, she didn't have much time to devote to her romantic interests, so she didn't follow up with them. When her life slows down, she plans to try the personals again using the same strategy and then focus more on following up with the promising men.

Like Ann and Liz, you too need to aim for compatibility and to look for those traits when reviewing the lists you create. But remember, while reviewing your list, don't edit yourself too far. Many times what is considered realistic is in the eyes of the beholder. Most people tend to match up with others of similar background, educational achievement, and even income level, but having confidence can expand a person's allure. Just strive to be like the person you want to attract and you'll attract the person you want to be with.

On the other hand, if many of the items on your lists from Chapter 3 describe attributes that are opposite of those that you described on the list in this chapter, ask yourself if you're trying to compensate for something. In *The Complete Idiot's Guide to Dating,* Dr. Judy Kuriansky writes that, "Opposites may at first attract, and then repel . . . the very traits that are endearing in the beginning of a relationship may be the same ones that drive you apart."

Choosing someone with opposite traits may seem like a practical way to fulfill certain needs. Often people marry others for this very reason. If someone is quiet, he or she may seek a more outgoing partner. And there are many other examples. It's just that if someone is trying to compensate for something through his or her mate, that person just needs to be aware of it, so he or she can work around any conflicts later.

And, finally, remember not to typecast your ideal partner. How many times have you spotted just your type in a bar or at a party? You move closer. You imagine his or her charm. The person smiles at you. You smile back. Nice clothes. Great body. Attractive face. You begin small talk. And then you discover something that isn't supposed to be in the picture. Your potential partner isn't perfect. All of a sudden the bubble bursts.

We all have preferences about physical traits. There's nothing wrong with that. And if all you want is a physical relationship, you shouldn't feel guilty about requesting only physical traits in your ad. But what if Toyota advertised its latest car as "perfect for the girl-next-door type"? How many buyers would tune out? Lots. If you ultimately want a serious relationship, requesting a certain physical type of person will limit your odds of finding the right person.

For instance, Melinda is a cute, educated, vibrant, creative woman. She has an incredible sense of humor and style. She always envisioned herself marrying a man with similar qualities. So who is she celebrating her 15th anniversary with? An average-looking, laid-back, but equally intelligent and fun-loving police officer. In other words, don't let your expectations limit your chances for happiness.

That doesn't mean you have to abandon your standards. After all, while some of us make the mistake of being too choosy, others aren't choosy enough. Many people settle for someone who lies, cheats, or fails to treat them with the respect they deserve. You may find that Mr. Perfect wants to engage in some sexual play you find distasteful. Or you suspect that Ms. Right has a drug problem. The bottom line is that accommodating differences should never make you feel degraded or guilty.

Listen to Yourself

Rich found a secretary in a neighboring office pleasant, bright, and extremely attractive. He planned on asking her out, but when he noticed her mustache, he was totally turned off.

Paula, after several pleasant dates with Joel, decided that he wasn't for her when he showed up in cowboy boots.

Both of these people realized that their change of heart was based on superficial factors. They knew that cowboy boots and female body hair had little to do with the person's potential as a mate. Furthermore, after already cultivating an interest in these people, they recognized how silly they were for the shift in attitude. Nevertheless both chose to end the relationship.

There are many possible causes for this type of behavior—such as fear of a relationship, issues with intimacy and trust, a judgmental personality, or the simple fact that a small trait just doesn't appeal to you. If you hear yourself being equally petty, ask yourself what's really going on. You may find that you're not ready for a relationship.

If you find that you are ready for a relationship, however, put your notes aside until Chapter 6. Now that you have a clear idea of the person you want to attract, you need to consider how best to reach him or her.

5

And Now 25 Words from Our Sponsor

The medium is the message.

—*Marshall McLuhan*

All right. You've decided to place an ad. You know the type of individual you want to meet and the type of relationship you want to have. You know how to describe yourself. You may even have an idea of what you want to say. So where should you place your ad? Think creatively, because the medium you choose is just as important in helping you reach your goals as what you say. In fact, it may even be more important. A good ad in the wrong place will fail, but an average ad, timed appropriately and in the right medium, can work wonders (your creative execution just makes it work that much more effectively). That's a guiding principle used by recruitment agencies who professionally develop want ads, and it's a principle you should use as well. After all, if your target doesn't see your ad, what good is it?

The good news is that you *do* have a multitude of options: newspapers, magazines, outdoor media (such as billboards and the sides of buses), bulletin boards in local retailers, and on-line computer services. In some areas, you can even use radio and cable television. Each medium has its benefits and trade-offs. But keep in mind that you don't have to use the medium the way you see it being employed by traditional advertisers. For instance, to use a billboard effectively, you don't need to look good in a bikini like a *Sports Illustrated* model; to use radio, you don't need a voice like James Earl Jones's.

So which medium should you use? The decision depends on you and what you've identified earlier. But to help you make your selection, we've identified the following eight considerations:

1. Timing: How quickly do you want your message to appear?
2. Geography: Where in the world would you like to find your partner?
3. Lifestyle: To what extent do you want your partner to live like you?
4. Demographics: Do you want your age, income, or educational levels to match?
5. Cost: How much do you want to spend?
6. Competition: Do you feel comfortable on a stage all your own or in a crowd?
7. Mechanics: How much production work do you want to do?
8. Presentation: How creative do you need to be with your ad to stand out from the crowd?

Let's look at each medium. We'll start with newspapers, because they're the most traditional and most popular place for personal ads. We'll then explore the other options in less detail, comparing them with newspaper ads. By combining this information with all of the soul-searching you've done earlier, your choice of medium should become obvious.

How Newspapers Can Help You Find Your Headliner

Weekly and daily newspapers carry the bulk of personal ads. There are several practical reasons for this: they're easy to use; they're the most traditional; and they offer more immediacy than most other forums— after all, newspapers are for reporting news. That's just what Patti discovered when she started dating through the personals.

Patti, in California, placed an ad in her local newspaper after answering a handful of ads in *Alaskan Man* (she had even corresponded with a few of the men but decided that she couldn't go further with them because of the physical distance). Since she'd heard that men in Los Angeles preferred women who weren't from California, she mentioned that she was from the Midwest. In addition, because she's six feet tall, she described herself accordingly. Her ad read:

> Statuesque, green-eyed, Midwestern blond SWF, 38, seeking intelligent, romantic, physically fit SWM with a sense of humor for weekend getaways.

She received about 50 responses. Many of the men seemed nice, but her schedule only allowed her to follow up with five of them. Patti scheduled a brief meeting with each man she'd selected, meeting him in a bar. One meeting, however, turned into an entertaining, six-hour conversation. That one was with Chuck, a 32-year-old Santa Barbara cartographer. Chuck and Patti started dating. Eventually they relocated together in Nevada. "You know," said Patti, "we're not romantically involved anymore, but he's still my best friend, and I know I've met my soul mate."

While you may not meet your soul mate through newspaper personals (no medium can guarantee that), you will find that they do offer an easy way to start dating. Running a personal ad in a newspaper is relatively inexpensive. Some even allow you to place the ad for free. When there is a fee, however, rates vary. Price can be based on the maintenance of a post office box for you, the size of your ad, or even the number of words you use. So if cost is a big factor for you, it's best to be concise.

Since newspaper personal ads are easily accessible and many people skim them out of curiosity or for amusement, you may actually attract the attention of a person who initially had no intention of responding. And because newspapers tend to have short production timelines and be read closer to their publication dates you may see results more quickly than with other media options.

Best yet, it doesn't take much for you to physically produce a newspaper classified ad. You don't need a background in art direction, a photographer, producer, director, or big budget. All you need is a pencil, paper, and possibly a thesaurus—plus the guidelines and considerations provided in this book.

How can you make the most of this medium? First, you need to decide in which newspaper you want your ad to appear. This depends on the type of person and relationship you're seeking. For example, if attending zydeco concerts or polka parties is a big part of how you like to spend your free time, there may be a music publication in your area that could help you find your mate. Or if you're into running, try a fitness publication.

Your motivation for placing the ad should also be considered. If you want dating mania, a daily newspaper or your local weekly entertainment giveaway is a good choice. That's because you'll need a publication with a large readership. But if you really want a conventional marriage, avoid the extreme alternative press and focus instead on publications that attract a more traditional readership; in this case, choose a daily or weekly newspaper that's more established.

Timing. As you probably realize, timing is a big factor in any successful dating situation—even dating through the personals. People tend to think about relationships more in the spring or before holidays such as Valentine's Day. But it may not be a good idea to have your ad appear right on the holiday or during the week between Christmas and New Year's Day, because a large number of singles are involved with their relatives and won't have the time to respond. Rather, you should place your ad several weeks before or after the holiday. You'll be able to line up dates for holiday parties or meet people when the postholiday breakups flood the singles scene.

Also, think about major upcoming sports events, concerts, elections—or even sales conferences. If you're seeking a football fan, he or she probably won't be paying much attention to personal ads on Super Bowl Sunday. It's better to place the ad several weeks before the event and mention your passion for the game in the body copy—and you might score before the event even starts. If you have concert tickets, advertise in advance for a date to accompany you.

What about waiting until the middle of winter? Since many people don't like to go out in the cold, they'll hesitate to respond to your ad. This will limit the number of letters or voice-mail messages you receive, which is good if you don't want to meet a person who is climatically challenged, but a detriment if you want to meet a large number of people.

As you can see, except for a few days, there is no right or wrong time of the year to run an ad. But there are better times for *you* to run one. It can help you better target your ad to your audience. What you need to do is plan when you want to date, and then work back to decide when you should run your ad.

If you want to work fast, however, newspapers provide you with more flexibility because lead times are so short. It may even be as short as a week—or less—from the time when you place your ad with the publication to when it appears. And you can begin receiving responses immediately after publication. To find the lead time for your newspaper, simply review the personal-ads section, or call the publication. Since the personal ads are a profit-generating device for the paper, the staff wants your ad and will go out of the way to help you place one.

Geography. Find the publications that are heavily distributed in your area. Why? Because as Lynn discovered, it's more convenient for you to date people who are near you. Think of it this way: You may love *The Village Voice* and believe that any one of its readers would be perfect for you. Great, if you live in New York; terrible if you live in Portland. Flying to Manhattan to meet a blind date for coffee isn't very practical. But placing a personal ad in a publication in another city may be practical if you travel there regularly. Our rule of thumb: neighborhood newspapers are a good bet because they'll put you in touch with people who are nearby. In larger urban areas, zoned editions of your daily newspaper are also a good bet—as well as established entertainment weeklies—just so long as you don't mind traveling to the areas. Remember, long commutes over time may create feelings of resentment, which can ultimately destroy a relationship.

Demographics. Find the publications that target your income level, living or working area, age group, and relationship status—and you will probably hook up with someone who resembles you—at least on the outside.

To show you the demographics in the personals, we edited an ad by Al, a successful managing director of a Midwest consulting firm. He turned to the personals 10 years ago because he spent so much time working that he wasn't able to meet women. "People don't have enough romantic opportunities to meet," he said. His view of the personals? "It's safer than the bars. And at the very least, you'll make new friends." So far, he's met dozens of women through ads in the *Chicago Reader,* a weekly newspaper with one of Chicago's largest singles sections and an educated younger audience. His current ad:

> Athletic SWM, 43, ISO attractive, slim, NS SF
> who enjoys good conversation, cats and dogs and
> fun times on my motorcycle.

To show you how you can meet people with similar demographic characteristics but with different interests (or lifestyle characteristics), we've edited Al's ad to read:

> Thoughtful SWM, 43, ISO attractive, NS SF
> who enjoys quiet times and serious books
> and movies. No pets, please.

As you can see, he's still a SWM who is 43 years old (the demographics), but his interests are different.

Just as ads target demographics in the copy, you should also target demographics in your choice of media. For newspapers, you should check to see if the readership fits the demographics you're seeking. But in applying this concept, remember that newspapers tend to define their demographics in very broad strokes. For success, try to match your interests and demographics as closely as possible with those of the publication's readership—or you'll possibly waste your time on people who don't interest you. After all, as you learned in Chapter 4, your similarities are one of your potential relationship's assets.

Lifestyle. Find the publications that interest you—that convey and mirror your viewpoints, interests, or activities—and you will probably meet someone who thinks like you do. The person will be like you on the inside. For an example of an ad with similar lifestyle characteristics but with different demographics, we have edited Al's ad again:

> Athletic SBM, 23, ISO attractive, suburban DF who enjoys good conversation, cats and dogs and fun times on my motorcycle.

As you can see, the interests are the same as Al's original ad (who he is on the inside), but the demographic characteristics are completely different. So when placing your ad, ask yourself, "Do I want to meet someone just like me—or someone who is the opposite of me?" Then use this information to help you select where to place your ad. (Our research, by the way, shows that couples who have a similar outlook on life but complement each other in personality traits are more successful, which means that you should use publications that generally reflect your lifestyle interests.)

Newspapers target a wide lifestyle range. They may be conservative or liberal, but only in general terms. An exception: ethnic or religious newspapers, such as those targeting Jewish, Catholic, Hispanic, or African-American people. Just keep in mind, when using an ethnic or religious publication, you'll attract responses from people whose backgrounds are important to them—and should be important to you as well. Since you'll reach an audience with a wider range of viewpoints, you'll have to work harder in your ad to target the type of person you want to meet. (The secrets of targeting via language usage will be discussed in the next chapter.)

Cost. The costs to you and your potential respondents are another consideration. These include the cost of producing your ad as well as responding to it. But you can use these factors to your advantage. For instance, you can use cost to help you gauge your respondents' income and motivational level. As we mentioned, newspapers tend to cost less than other forms of media. Consequently, newspaper advertisers may be less determined to find a match or they may have less income.

But there are differences among newspapers as well. A publication that requires your respondent to make an expensive call to a 900-number will discourage people with lower incomes or those who are less motivated. A more expensive newspaper may also be right for you if regular trips to Neiman Marcus or Saks Fifth Avenue are important to you. But if spending big bucks is not important to you or if you want to get a greater number of responses, go the least expensive route.

Competition. Imagine that your potential love interest picks up a publication crammed with pages of personal ads. What are the chances that he or she will read every single ad? Our research says the odds are poor. You might have better luck in a medium that has a more limited personal-ad section—unless you can afford six column inches to attract attention or you're able to create a message that really stands out. (For creative strategies, see Chapter 6.)

Since newspaper personals tend to cost less than those in other media, your competition will be greater, requiring you to work harder to get attention. Some personal-ad sections will, for an extra charge, allow a bold headline or border around your ad. This may help. But if your words alone can't attract your Mr. or Ms. Right, we recommend you don't run your ad in a newspaper.

Mechanics. Newspaper ads are the easiest to produce. Depending on the publication in your area, you have two options in taking out an ad—you can call or write. When writing, unless your handwriting is very neat, simply type your copy—because you wouldn't want readers to think you're "blind" when what you meant to say was "blond"—or vice versa. A typo in the ad can definitely alter the quality of the responses you receive. For instance, while we did not talk with anyone whose life was changed due to a typo, an article on personal ads in the April 1997 edition of *Redbook* mentioned that a man was not going to respond to an ad because he thought the woman was too young for him; in reality, the age listed in the woman's ad was wrong, which he discovered to his delight when he responded anyway, found that she was only one year younger than he, and eventually married the woman. Just imagine if he'd let what was actually a typo stop him!

Once your ad has been carefully proofread, submit it to the paper. And voilà! Instant dating—*if* your ad has the punch that you'll learn to create in the next chapter.

If you have big bucks, you may want to buy space for a traditional ad with a headline, a visual (containing either a photo or an illustration), as well as body copy. These are called display ads. And although we haven't seen anyone use them yet for dating purposes, they may help you attract attention and beat your competition. However, you must be careful that you're not confused with a dating service, because they buy display space to advertise their services. As we'll see in our section on outdoor advertising, any confusion with a dating service will lower, or may even wipe out completely, the number of responses you get.

Presentation. Let's face it, unless you take the drastic step of buying a display ad, your impact in the newspaper is limited to what you can accomplish with words. So what kinds of words and language best fit you? Are you prone to using descriptors that require your friends to bring along a dictionary? Or are adjectives like *cool* more your style? These are issues we'll discuss in the next chapter and will be the factors in bringing about success in any publication filled with ads.

Keep in mind that most newspapers and magazines maintain policies giving them the power to reject your ad if it is deemed inappropriate for their publication. To avoid any potential trouble, check with the publication you're considering before you create your ad to make sure they'll run it.

Using Magazines to Increase Your Circulation

Magazine advertising offers a good way to reach specific audiences. Do you want your man to read *Field & Stream* or *Forbes*? Does your ideal woman subscribe to *Good Housekeeping, Cosmopolitan,* or *Business Week*?

If you have a pot full of money, you could buy space in almost any magazine—even perhaps, on the inside cover of *Time!* Although most national magazines don't have a section dedicated to personal ads (requiring you to purchase a display ad if you pass their policy on appropriateness), most regional and special-interest magazines *do* run personals. Plus, many publications that don't have a personal-ad section, including some national magazines, do allow personal ads in their general classified sections.

Their benefit? They're generally more homogeneous. They have less competition. And most of all, they really work!

With an open mind and fully recovered from the breakup of a five-year marriage, Audry decided she was ready for a meaningful relationship and decided to try the personals. But where? *The Village Voice* is known for having one of the most established personal-ad sections in New York, but she was afraid that the average *Village Voice* reader wouldn't possess the intelligence, values, and ability to commit to the type of relationship that she wanted, so she chose *New York* magazine instead. It carried a significant personal-ad section and was read by New York's more upscale professionals. With her ad, she hoped to attract a man with interests and values in common with her own, or at least one who was solvent and stable. Here's her ad:

> Sells computers, sings jazz. Jewish female, 31, slim, pretty, seeks creative, fit, courageous man to share NYC music and maybe the "C" word.

You may have heard that love appears in the most unexpected places. How about in a garbage bin in an alley? You just have to keep an open mind. Right? Because that is just what happened. Ben, a busy New York actor, was walking his neighbor's dog when he saw a copy of the

New York magazine that had Audry's ad. It was sitting on top of the recycling bin. As he was reading the magazine, Audry's ad caught his eye because he also enjoyed jazz and computers. Plus, he felt that Audry might be a cut above average, because of the publication she had used to place her ad.

Even though the magazine's six-week window for responses was about to close, Ben decided to send off a note. Audry liked what he had to say, called him, and they started dating. Exactly one year later, while on their motorcycles in a busy New York intersection, Ben proposed marriage. Audry accepted and they've been together ever since.

Perhaps your story won't revolve around a garbage bin, but you might just meet that special someone through the personals section of a magazine. So here are some considerations to think through before placing your ad:

Timing. Unlike newspapers, there is a longer lead time with magazines. Most magazines are assembled months ahead of their publication dates and are not fully read for six weeks after that (this includes time-sensitive publications like newsmagazines). So if you're seeking a date for a week from Saturday night, magazines are not your best choice. But if you plan ahead, they can provide many benefits. Your ad will appear in a higher-quality publication and, as we said earlier, your target audience will be more homogeneous. An added bonus is that in most cases, you will have less competition.

Geography. If you plan on using a magazine, we recommend a local or regional one, unless you've saved up your pennies and your frequent flyer miles. The most common are location-based magazines, such as *Chicago* or *New York* magazine. Some national magazines have sections that are printed in regional editions, but these will give you a lower response rate simply because they are not used as often.

Demographics. Magazines are also a very good way to target a specific audience—people within a certain age range or income level. To find the demographic information on the magazine you're considering, contact the publication. Tell the advertising sales rep that you're interested in buying ad space and ask for circulation information. Combine the demographic and lifestyle information you get about the magazine's readers and you can easily predict the types of people you'll meet. The only magazines that will not allow you to predict the type of people you will meet are those dedicated solely to publishing personal ads. In these publications, you only have your words to target people, requiring a creative strategy similar to the one used for newspapers, and success depends on the weeding-out process after you get your responses.

Lifestyle. Targeting lifestyle characteristics is one of the best reasons to use magazine advertising. Chances are your magazine's audience has a lot in common with you. And the more narrow the audience, the better your chances. If, for instance, you place an ad in *Chicago* magazine, you'll likely encounter people with a taste for upscale living and the cultural events in the Chicago area—lifestyle characteristics that you may share. If you place an ad in *Chicago Mac-Users,* you've narrowed the playing field even more.

Paul, a sound engineer and musician, was new to his town and eager to connect with people like him. One of his interests was industrial music, so he placed this ad in *Industrial Nation,* an international underground music publication.

I am a 24-year-old heterosexual male living just outside of New York and frustrated by the natives here being so unfriendly and hard to hook up with. (Why the f*** do big city people have to be this way???) My interests include (but are by no means limited to) Skinny Puppy, Einsturzende Neubauten, Cocteau Twins, Severed Heads, Coil Wire, Controlled Bleeding, Click Click, Sisters of Mercy, Depeche Mode, The Cure, Terry Gilliam movies, *Star Trek,* H. R. Giger, Ralph Steadman, *Aliens* (the movie as well as the life forms), Edgar Allen Poe, Akira, demented animation, and infinitely more. So if you are out there and ready to remind me that there is more to this city than snotty yuppies and obnoxious gangstas, please write. Time does not stand still, and neither do I . . .

Not exactly an ad you'd find in *Martha Stewart's Living*, but it generated about 20 responses—some from as far away as Copenhagen. Although Paul was open to forming connections with males and females from anywhere, ultimately he wanted his ad to attract a woman for a long-term relationship. He chose *Industrial Nation* because its unique lifestyle chracteristics were so in tune with his own.

The ad pulled responses from like-minded people from Dallas, Los Angeles, New York, Chicago, Flagstaff, and a number of other cities. Paul did his best to create pen-pal relationships and even kept in touch through numerous e-mails over several months, but soon decided to narrow his correspondence to those who didn't require an airline ticket to visit.

While Paul was correct in targeting interest, he did so by ignoring the geographic considerations. In any medium, the best mix of all eight considerations will work best for you.

Cost. Magazine space costs more than newspaper space—as much as three times more. However, this may enable you to attract a more discriminating shopper—and possibly a partner who is more interested in a long-term relationship.

Competition. You have less competition with a magazine personal-ad section because, simply stated, the high cost allows fewer people to use them. The exception to this is, of course, the magazines geared solely to publishing personal ads, which are crammed with ads from specific regions. But in those publications not only is there more competition, but your audience is less targeted, requiring your personal ad to work harder.

Mechanics. Putting a magazine ad together is the same as putting one together for a newspaper and is dependent upon each publication's specifications. We recommend you contact the specific publication for information.

Presentation. You have the same constraints in creating your ad for a magazine as you do with a newspaper ad. So unless you are investing in a quarter-page display ad, get out your thesaurus and start looking up all those great descriptors.

A Sign of Love: Meeting Your Mate Through an Outdoor Ad

Imagine you're driving down the highway when all of a sudden an attractive woman on a billboard catches your eye. She looks fun-loving and intelligent. But she's not a model. And she is not selling Jim Beam or Buicks. Instead, she's interested in finding a guy who is as gutsy as she is! Yes, this medium has been used for finding mates. No, you don't have to put your face on a billboard. You can maintain your anonymity and still be effective. For instance:

> 4 Professional, Middle-Class Women
> Ages 29–31, Seek Husbands.

Emily got the idea to use billboards to place her personal ad from one she saw in San Antonio. With four of her friends, she rented four billboards located on major Chicago thoroughfares. The cost was $650 for three months. The response? Nothing—that is until the press started giving them publicity, which is just what they'd counted on. They were interviewed on major radio stations and were the subject of feature articles, which helped them generate more than 500 responses, including 100 from the Philippines, as well as some from Germany and France. Ninety percent of the responses from their area were professionals.

The only way to handle the volume was to be very methodical. First, they screened the letters and held individual one-hour interviews back-to-back on weekends with 150 of the men. Then they hosted a party for all the interviewees and single women they could find. The result: About 50 people met and dated after that night; some would later marry.

Ross, in Florida, also tried the billboard approach. He made 14 cardboard signs and placed them on Florida's well-traveled highways near his home in Tampa:

Wife Wanted. Call Ross at 555-555-5555.

This retired 46-year-old had been married for 22 years and had a 14-year-old son. He said that after his divorce it took him a few years to rejoin the dating scene. But Ross didn't like to go to bars. So he tried billboards. At first he used a professional sign service to create his billboards, but respondents assumed that he was offering a dating service. He changed to his more rustic presentation, and there was no mistaking that the signs were placed by an individual.

Ross received about 350 calls—about a quarter of which came after API had picked up his story and aired it across the country. Excluding the responses generated by publicity, why did Ross get more calls from his homemade signs than Emily got from her professionally produced and placed signs? Because they looked like they were created by an individual—rather than looking like they were from a dating service—so he didn't have to depend on the outside media to give him credibility.

These stories demonstrate a valuable lesson: a unique use of media can help draw attention—from both individuals and the press, which will then dramatically increase the number of responses you receive. Another important consideration: billboards are more intrusive, enabling you to attract the attention of people who don't actively read the personals. So by using them, you're halfway there in attracting an elusive yet desirable dating partner.

Another medium, one that closely resembles billboards, are the bulletin boards that you find in your local retailers (not to be confused with electronic bulletin boards that we discuss later in this chapter). Simply ask the proprietor of the store if you can place your message. If there's room and the proprietor doesn't have an issue with the content, he or she generally will allow it to go up.

Timing. Billboards offer a wider window of opportunity than most other media. That's because of two factors: first, billboards tend to be up for weeks or even months and second, people tend to travel the same route each day, giving the potential Mr. or Ms. Right of your life more opportunities to decide to call or write. But since the number of professionally produced billboards is limited in any particular area and they may be reserved months in advance, you may have to plan ahead to get the spot you want—unless you luck out and find a billboard that has not been reserved.

The best way to use this medium is to first identify the billboard you want to rent. Then simply look on, or near, the billboard's frame to see the name of the company that manages it. Or you can look in the yellow pages under outdoor advertising and call for available locations. Sales reps can help you determine a good location and, if necessary, guide you in your presentation.

Geography. Location is critical. Where your billboard or bulletin board is located has a major impact on the quantity and quality of responses. Logically, if your billboard is in an out-of-the-way place—such as down a dead-end street in an industrial park—or if your bulletin board is in a store that's not very successful, not too many people will see it. However, if it's along a highly traveled expressway or in a popular spot, many people will see it, but perhaps they won't have the time to jot down your phone or post office box number. A good alternative is a well-traveled city street, preferably with pedestrian traffic or near a stoplight, so people will see your message, find it easy to read, and have time to take down your address. For bulletin boards, try a coffee shop, book store, or any other popular place people like to hang out.

Demographics. Billboards and bulletin boards allow you to target specific demographic groups because people who live in the same neighborhood often share income and educational levels. For instance, since most singles don't live in suburban subdivisions, placing a bulletin board notice or billboard in such areas would be inadvisable. But placing a billboard ad next to a singles apartment complex—or a note on the complex's message center—has great potential. Also, consider using a billboard near the major dating section of town, e.g., restaurant row.

Lifestyle. With a billboard, you won't have a great opportunity to target your message to a group with a particular interest—unless, of course, it is located in an area that is made up of extremely homogeneous neighborhoods. However, you will have this opportunity to target if you use a bulletin board ad—just place it in a store that caters to a specific interest, such as camping or exercising.

Cost. Billboards aren't cheap. But keep in mind that costs can vary greatly depending on the area and artwork you choose. Renting a downtown billboard with a full-color picture of two people running through a meadow will impact your pocketbook substantially more than two lines of black type stating your interests and your post office box number (which, of course, is another cost, because you'll have to rent one if you want to maintain your anonymity).

Bulletin board ads, however, are inexpensive. All they'll cost you is the paper you use, computer time (if you want to desktop publish it and don't own one), and the most important item, a post office box in which to collect your responses.

Competition. What competition? With a billboard, you're out there on your own—except for a few signs that are promoting beer and cigarettes. This is both its biggest plus and its greatest weakness because many people may not take it as a serious opportunity. With bulletin boards, it all depends on the number of messages around yours; but remember that most of these messages will not be for getting dates, so your direct competition should be slim.

Mechanics. Some billboard companies ask for camera-ready art, which means your ad is exactly as you want it to be printed. Others just need a rough doodle and they'll do the rest. Since most billboard companies don't want to lose any business, they will help you out if you don't happen to have a fully staffed design studio at your disposal. For bulletin boards, just type it up or desktop publish it, unless you have neat handwriting and want to create an extremely homespun feeling.

Presentation. Any outdoor message should be quick and to the point. The guideline is to use less than seven words in rural and suburban areas, because people are speeding by. In urban neighborhoods with stop-and-go traffic, people have more time to read, so you can use a few more words. You should make sure that your message is credible. If you want to spend bigger bucks and have some fun with your quest to find a mate, you may want to try a sequential method, several boards or posters in a row, like the old Burma Shave signs. Of course, the more signs, the more money or work—but they'll also attract more attention!

On-Line Love: The Story Behind True Computer Dating

After her divorce, Tracy, 32, moved to the big city to return to school and begin enjoying the single life. But between working part-time and earning her graduate degree in marketing, she didn't have time to socialize as much as she liked. It took her about a year to realize that she needed some help meeting men.

She signed up with America Online. It was easier, cheaper, and more convenient for her to venture on-line to chat with men than it was for her to go to bars. She enjoyed the spontaneity. She could gauge potential love interests' educational levels or intelligence by their ability to spell and put grammatically correct sentences together. And she figured that anyone who could navigate the complexities of on-line services had to have some intelligence.

Tracy took advantage of the medium's immediacy. If after a long conversation she had enough information to feel safe, she met the man the same day in a nearby restaurant. At other times, Tracy spoke on the phone over the course of weeks—and even months—before meeting. In fact, within a few months she had chatted with about 150 men, which led to dates with more than 20 of them. And she began to enjoy the single life!

Because so many people like Tracy have invested in a home computer and modem, the on-line dating world has exploded. You don't have to go anywhere. You don't have to spend money. You're able to target specific groups.

There are two methods of using this medium. Most on-line services, such as America Online (AOL) and CompuServe, have abundant chat rooms, where you type in comments and often receive an immediate response from individuals in the group. It's like going to a bar to meet someone: the type of crowd depends on the kind of chat room you're in. Typically, there are between 15 and 50 people in a chat room.

If you develop a rapport with someone, you can engage in more direct conversation through instant messaging offered by most servers. This feature allows you to chat privately with the individual. It's like being at a party and taking someone out of a group discussion for one-to-one conversation. Instant messages are not monitored, so you can say whatever you like.

On-line services also host electronic bulletin boards, where you can leave messages for an unlimited number of people. Replies are left on the bulletin board, which you can read when you return on-line. Respondents can also e-mail you directly. Bulletin board servers dedicated solely to personal ads are also available. These function like personal ads in a newspaper, but there is one big important difference: using the on-line service's member directory, you can check if the advertiser or respondent is compatible. The directory is a database of information that often includes age, marital status, location, hobbies, and birth date. This can be a valuable resource. (Newspaper companies are also taking out websites for their publications, allowing people to find traditional personal ads on the Internet. But these should not be confused with bulletin boards, because traditional placement and response methods are still required. Perhaps as the technology evolves, you will be able to place and respond to them on-line.)

The difference between a live chat room and a bulletin board is like the difference between walking into a bar and placing an ad in a newspaper. Both methods require a strategy, but you need a different set of skills to be successful at each.

Live Chat Method

Timing. Fast, fast, fast. If you need a date for tonight, a chat room might help you find one. But it's probably not very safe to meet "Rat-dog" on-line at 4 A.M. and go on a first date that evening. In Chapter 9 of this book, there's important advice on protecting yourself during dates. But the first step in any dating situation is to use common sense. So find out to whom you're actually talking before you meet him or her in person.

Geography. As with other media, your willingness to travel determines your ad's placement. You can access a local chat room and get in touch with someone living on the next block. But if you are using the Internet and have an upcoming business trip to Stockholm, you may also be able to line up a dinner date there.

Demographics. Until as many people have computers as have telephones, on-line dating offers you access to a unique demographic group. Obviously, because computers are not inexpensive, your audience has a higher average income than the general population. The group is more interested in technology as well. On-line you'll meet a higher number of engineers, computer professionals, or people in the sciences than you will find in the general population.

These demographics are changing quickly though, so make sure the technically astute person you are chatting with isn't an 11-year-old. You can't tell age—or any other personal features—over the Internet. Also keep in mind that since this medium is one of the most immediate and least regulated, it is also one of the most likely to allow for security lapses.

Lifestyle. Many chat rooms focus on specific interests. They are your best bet for meeting people whose interests are the same as yours. Rooms exist for gays, people over 40, under 30, Jewish, and a host of other categories. But keep in mind, if you access a special-interest chat room, you'll meet married people there, too. (If one of the people in the room, however, is single, you may be in luck.) Also remember that because on-line interaction is so anonymous, people often say things they wouldn't ordinarily say to someone face-to-face.

Cost. Aside from the cost of the computer and on-line service, what you spend can depend on how long you stay on-line. Most on-line services offer a number of hours free with the packages. After that time is used, subscribers are charged by the hour. Internet providers offer a variety of similar plans, and most also offer flat-fee, unlimited-use plans as well.

Competition. The amount of competition depends on the number of people in your chat room. Most rooms host about 15 to 50 people. If you've been talking for a while and nothing happens, move to another room. However, in any live chat forum, your ability to beat the competition depends on your ability to be a good conversationalist. Start new topics. Be witty. Greet the group. Live chat is where the extroverts have the edge.

Mechanics. The mechanics here have more to do with baud rates (i.e., the speed at which your modem can transmit information) than print line counts. Also make sure you can spell. (But if you do misspell something, just acknowledge it so you don't look like a moron.) Don't use all caps either; it means you are yelling on-line. And it doesn't hurt to work on your typing speed so that you can more quickly enter your comments.

Presentation. OK, it's live chat. Have something pertinent to say and keep your favorite jokes handy. If you're interested in sports, be able to talk about what's going on. If politics fascinates you, start a conversation that will attract comments. Use emoticons, symbols such as :) (a happy face), to give your remarks more personality (see Appendix B for more emoticons you can use). Think of yourself at a cocktail party, and act accordingly. A good guideline is to avoid saying anything you wouldn't hear on network television. And, as anyone who's ever spent significant time on-line knows, there is a unique sense of etiquette. Be mindful of it.

Computer Bulletin Boards

Timing. Bulletin boards are for people who want Cupid to shoot an arrow into the air and see what happens. Guidelines for when to use a bulletin board for an ad are about the same as for other forms of media. Avoid times like the holidays when people are busy. Weather considerations are another factor; people are more apt to sit down at their computers when it's cold or rainy outside than they would on a beautiful summer day.

Most serious bulletin board users don't pay much attention to old messages, especially when it comes to personal ads. People may think that if you placed the message 10 months ago and you're still available, either your notice is outdated or you're probably not much of a catch. So if you plan on using the bulletin board method to meet someone, replace your message every two months—or more often.

Should you change your screen name when you change your ad? No. Otherwise, you may attract the same people you didn't connect with the first time around. You may again have to reject that same incompatible connection. Be current, not dishonest.

The goal of placing a second bulletin board personal ad is to catch the eye of people who missed your first one, or to refine your ad to play up qualities you missed in your first round.

Geography. Like live chat rooms, bulletin board systems are operated locally, nationally, and internationally. For purely practical reasons, it makes sense to post your ad in a local file, so you won't need an expensive airline ticket just to meet the respondent.

Demographics. Users of computer bulletin boards tend to have higher incomes and are better educated than the general population. However, they tend to be older than those who turn to the chat room. More important, since bulletin boards more closely resemble the personal ads from the print media, you're more likely to meet someone who is focused on forming a traditional relationship (rather than just the on-line romances chat rooms inspire).

Lifestyle. Within the universe of computer users, people have a wide range of interests and opinions. But because there are so many bulletin boards targeted to specific groups, it's easy to find someone who shares your interests.

Cost. There are no costs to posting a personal ad on your server's bulletin board beyond your normal on-line fees. Internet sites devoted strictly to personal ads, however, sometimes have a monthly membership fee.

Competition. Competition is fierce! Since it's not uncommon for a bulletin board to contain as many as 10,000 simultaneous postings, your challenge is to use every chance you have to get noticed. One opportunity is the screen name you choose. If, for example, you follow a sport and want to find others with the same interest, you should select a name that will draw their attention, e.g., *CubsLovr.* But be sensitive to nuance and the possibility of misinterpretation. *BallLovr* may spark an avalanche of lewd comments. And remember that while a seductive screen name might be all you're trying to accomplish, you'll definitely attract people with only one thing on their minds.

Mechanics. An advantage to on-line personals is that you don't even need a postage stamp or a neatly printed ad submission, bright colors, or charming photos. However, you must make sure your spelling is checked, so you don't appear illiterate. Unlike a live chat room, you have an opportunity to put some thought into your message. Remember that once you post a bulletin board ad, it's up there.

When posting an ad on-line, it's also important to make sure the site is easy to find. Don, a former talk-show host who currently is a CEO and consultant in Arizona, discovered this when he decided that he was ready to settle down and, to meet someone, placed the profile on the next page on-line with his photo.

While Don is an interesting, accomplished, attractive man, he received just one response and it was from a woman whose commute would have taken the edge off the romance. That may be because Don's personal ad appeared in a seldom-advertised section of his on-line service. And because, at this point, men outnumber women in the on-line arena, he needed to go where there was more traffic. By listing his information in several spots—or in more traveled locations—he could have increased his response rate.

Presentation. Until graphics and video play a bigger role in on-line services, most electronic bulletin board ads rely on words. Currently, you can't even put little hearts or bold copy as you might in a newspaper ad. So your words are more important here than in almost any other media. Be specific in describing what you want and who you are. (If you have a scanner and are not concerned with anonymity, you can even scan your photo and file it in an on-line photo library or send it to anyone who inquires about your appearance.) Since many on-line subscription services monitor the messages left on their bulletin boards, please keep it clean. If you don't, you won't be the first subscriber to receive a letter suspending your service because of obscene language.

```
        Member Name: Don
           Location: Arizona
                Sex: Male
     Marital Status: Divorced, one great daughter.
            Hobbies: Flying airplanes, gliders & kites;
                     gourmet cooking; travel (physical
                     and metaphysical); people; home
                     building; friends; golf; football;
                     NCAA  nal 4; NBA Championships;
                     World Series; culture; writing;
                     wishing on stars; more . . .
         Occupation: CEO family and legal support
                     services corp. Business consultant.
                     Entrepreneur.
              Likes: Jocundity, gusto, sweet hearts,
                     simplicity
           Dislikes: Forms like this, which are too
                     short to be accurate
     Good Qualities: Great kisser, World-class hugs,
                     Peter Pan's friend
         Bad Habits: Do too much; poor, poor mate
                     selection; gullible

With a million dollars, I would . . .
Make sure my daughter was secure. Pay bills. Laugh
my ass off.
Tired of being alone; ready, willing, and able.
Magni cent heart. Super partner. Intellectual,
spiritual, eclectic, LOVE TO LAUGH, CUDDLE.
```

Radio: Helping You Put Love in the Air

The sound of lips kissing. Your favorite romantic tune. While radio stations might not have gone so far as to include spots for on-air personal ads, many have begun to offer single listeners a 900-number as a forum to meet people. This is a good way to target a large group that is culturally, or at least musically, compatible with you.

How does it work? The radio station contracts with a telecommunications company that handles the callers. The service's toll-free 800- or 888-number is publicized on the air. When you call to enroll, you do not speak to customer service; rather, a recording of a favorite radio personality walks you through the enrollment process. You answer questions regarding age range, location, marital status, education, personal habits such as smoking, religious preferences, and many other dating factors. In most cases the questionnaire was designed by social scientists, and a computer codes the data to identify possible matches. Everything you enter is absolutely confidential, of course, and it is not as intimidating as speaking to a live rep because you just need to select your answers from a menu.

You record your greeting message during the telephone enrollment. The entire process takes about seven minutes from start to finish. If you want to call customer service for tips on how to leave a good message, you can. The customer service reps usually can help with any questions members have about how to use the system effectively. Once you complete your greeting, it's screened by a customer service rep for bad language, overly suggestive remarks, or other comments that may be distasteful to members.

The computer matches the data with other members and presents matches to the members by placing their greetings in the members' mailboxes. The computer also has the flexibility to identify a near match. For example, if you specify an age range and a near match has all the qualities you want—except the age is a few years off—the computer will present the match anyway. In other words, the computer scans the ads for you.

Like placing a message, calling to find out how many dates and messages you have is also free, through the toll-free line. You are only charged when you call to find out more about your matches or exchange voice-mail messages with them. When you call to find out more about your matches, you will hear each individual's personal profile as well as his or her greeting message. Then you can leave him or her a voice-mail message if you want.

Timing. A radio station's date line can connect you with other people very quickly. As soon as your profile is logged in the computer, it begins matching. Listening to the radio station is a good guide to learning when its date line might have more traffic—which could mean a quicker route to a match. If the station is sponsoring a big event, there may be more people listening, and therefore possibly more date-line members signing up.

Geography. The area a radio date line covers is only limited by the radio station's range. A smaller station has a smaller range; a larger station covers a wider area. However, the cumulative listenership is more of an indicator than the range in terms of the number of people you'll be exposed to. A station could have many listeners in an urban area, say Houston, versus fewer listeners spread out over the rest of Texas.

Demographics. Radio station listeners are likely to have a lot in common. They are probably of similar age and location. Marital status, income, and educational level will of course vary. Also, the more popular the station, the more potential people in the date-line database. (Members must be at least 18.)

Lifestyle. Unlike most daily newspapers, a radio station's audience often shares a similar attitude or outlook. Listeners may tune into only that one country, alternative, classical, or classic rock music station, but they may all read the same newspaper. So if a certain type of music is important to you, you've got a good chance of finding compatible people through a station's date line.

Cost. There are no up-front costs to placing a personal ad with a radio station date line, but callers are charged for placing and retrieving messages. Fees, which are charged to your phone bill, can be as high as several dollars per minute, so it's important to be brief.

Competition. Although a radio station may handle thousands of callers each month, since the computer sorts the messages, competition is lessened. The bigger challenge is making your greeting the one the member answers when there are 20 potential dates in his or her mailbox.

Mechanics. All you need to enroll in a radio station's date line is a phone . . . although a radio might help, too!

Creative. When it comes to radio date lines, singles with luscious, seductive voices have the edge. You can also record your greeting with your favorite music in the background. Whatever you decide to say, be sure to practice, not read, your greeting, so it's natural and smooth. Be considerate of members' budgets and keep both your greeting and messages as short as possible.

Our Dim View of Cable Television

On first glance, television seems to offer many benefits to the dating world: you can combine sound and movement to express your message. So should you use it? Not yet. With the growth of cable TV and its need to find new ways of tying into its community, this medium is becoming a possibility, but because television personals are not very developed yet, there are drawbacks.

Breaking into this medium requires an extra effort just to learn the ropes. The production costs alone should discourage most people. Even then, because it's new to the medium, your message may not be interpreted as a personal ad.

So what are its benefits (besides allowing you to combine sound and movement)? Cable television is highly selective, allowing you to target your local community. In fact, an ad running on a local cable channel won't be seen beyond your viewing area—unless you ask that it be run in another location. Slightly less selective, but also giving you the opportunity to reach your community, are the local broadcast channels.

In some markets, there are cable television shows dedicated to dating through the personals. But so far they're pretty tacky. So you might not want to be seen on one of them. For instance, one cable program ran personal ads and had models walk down a runway in a disco atmosphere straight out of the '70s. Standing near the side, an announcer described the participants' features while a 900-number flashed over the screen. Not exactly the dignity you'd like bestowed in this sensitive situation.

And even though *The Dating Game* is back on the air and MTV has created *Singled Out,* these programs are outside the realm of advertising because the single person is not the sponsor. Plus, the major network affiliates currently have commercial standards boards that require all advertising to meet certain criteria in order to purchase airtime.

However, as personal ads continue to gain in popularity, they may offer cable television stations many promotional opportunities. So we think it's only a matter of time before television personal ads become commonplace. Once this medium develops and more people watch cable-access channels, running personal ads on television may bring successful results. Meanwhile, stay with the other media we've mentioned—and you can easily maintain your dignity.

As you can see, your media choices are only limited by your own creativity—and finances. If you want to meet someone, there is a medium for you. Before you take out an ad, we recommend that you study your chosen medium carefully. This will not only help you better use your ad, it can help you protect yourself by learning what to expect.

Now for the fun stuff! In the next chapter, we'll take you through actually creating your message and, if need be, your art and spots.

6

New and Improved
Singles Jingles

It don't mean a thing if it ain't got that swing.

—Duke Ellington

Let's take a little test. It's easy. Don't worry, we won't grade you. We'll ask you to think like a reader of personal ads. In one case, think like a male; in the other, think like a female. In the first case, it's a man, 26, who enjoys playing golf and tennis and wants to meet a woman who shares his interests but doesn't want to settle down. One day, he decides to scan the personals of his local weekly newspaper. It's chockfull of ads. If you were him, which one of the following ads would more likely grab your attention?

> Attractive SWF, 24, who enjoys playing participatory sports seeks sports-minded SWM 22–30 to share our mutual interests.

> Spice up your game w/Helen Hunt-type SWF, 24, for matches on the green or tennis court with SWM, 22–30, of warmth and wit who is also into rock, restaurants, and reels of classic and new films. Tennis, anyone?

Now, in this next case, a female is reading a local magazine. She comes across the personal ads and starts to read. Which man do you think she would be more interested in meeting?

> SWM, 26, 5'10", 170, seeks
> SWF, 22–30 for golf, tennis, evenings
> out and casual relationship.

> Casual game of golf or tennis?
> SWM, 26, 5'10", 170, seeks SWF, 22–30,
> partner to pamper for casual dating and
> dining. If you dress casually, call.

Granted, in both cases, the first ad would probably generate some responses—if the timing was right and it was placed in the right medium. But according to our research, more people in each case would be drawn to and intrigued by the second ad. That's because, in each case, the person of the second ad came across as more of an individual. He or she had specific interests, conveyed a unique personality, and indicated that he or she had a sense of fun. And while it typically takes a few more words to accomplish this, the investment and the effort are well worth it.

In both examples the first ad didn't truly represent the individual or show him or her in the best light. It's like meeting someone in a sports bar and limiting your conversation to the football game that's being broadcast. It probably wouldn't bring the results you want—or at least wouldn't bring the results very efficiently. A fairly standard, uninspired ad may indicate to readers that you're a fairly standard, uninspired individual, perhaps even boring. And if it's surrounded by ads that are more interesting than yours, your ad could become lost in the clutter and the people you want to meet may miss what you have to say.

Why did we give this test? Because that's the same test that you'll have to give your ad once you've written it. The more creative you can make your ad, the more likely it is that your message will be noticed. Right, you say, that's more easily said than done; the most creative thing I've ever accomplished was building a working volcano for my fifth-grade science class.

But everyone is creative in at least one part of his or her life. It's just human nature. So it's really not hard to create a more interesting ad. Just tap into your natural energy and follow our suggestions. We'll reveal a strategy for targeting your audience through your headline, take you through the word-choice considerations you need to make, as well as give pointers for developing ads for nontraditional media. At the end of the chapter, you'll find a handy, easy-to-use checklist, enabling you to test your ad for completeness and effectiveness before publishing it.

We recommend that you read the rest of the chapter before you start writing your ad, because it will help take the mystery out of crafting an effective one. Then go back and work through the exercises. Whatever you do, remember to take your time with the writing process because once you've completed that step, you'll be ready to roll!

Our Recipe for Romance

When you write your ad, don't wait for inspiration. Start working and inspiration will come to you. That's because it's really simple to write a personal ad—if you've been following our process. Just make sure your ad describes:

1. Who you are (the hard facts—including age and race—as well as your personality)
2. The person you desire (again, include lifestyle and demographic characteristics)
3. What type of relationship you want (we don't want to be misleading now, do we?)

Of course, none of this should be a surprise after what you've learned so far. Start with the words that you generated in the exercises in Chapters 2 through 4: the words that describe you, your ideal partner, and the type of relationship you want. Try to keep it simple and make it a very straightforward ad. While this may sound obvious, it's amazing to see the number of personal ads missing pertinent and fairly important information that would have boosted the response rate. For example, say you're a 42-year-old man, who likes golf and wants to meet a woman who also plays golf for fun times on the weekend. You can write something like:

> SWM, 42, seeks SWF, 40–45 for
> weekend golf outings, perhaps more.

This ad, although simple and direct, when placed in the right media, should get responses. That's because a well-written, straightforward ad that's pertinent to your target audience will get more responses than a highly creative ad that's vague. Of course, you'll probably want to make your ad work harder to attract a person with more specific qualities. And you can—once you've written your first draft. The point is to get the facts down first; then be creative. That way you can be sure that you've included all of the information you want to cover.

Once your ad has been written, study it. And start playing with the ideas in it. For instance, in the fictional ad you just read, the writer may start playing with the wording and generate a headline like, "A Hole in One." This would indicate his interest in golf as well as hint that he or the type of relationship he has to offer is a rare find, or perhaps that this ad is the only one that a woman would need to answer. Of course, the copy would then have to be reworked to substantiate and reinforce these claims.

You may want to test your straightforward ad before trying to make it more creative. Gabe ran his straightforward ad and got positive results. As a recently divorced, recently relocated, single parent, this regional manager for a mortgage corporation wanted to meet someone special but had found few opportunities to make this happen. Inspired by a friend who'd met and married through the personals, he thought he'd try it using a straightforward approach. He wrote:

> Professional DBM, college educated, articulate, handsome,
> fit, very outgoing and adventurous. Seeking professional, slim,
> S/DWF, 24–36, who enjoys aerobics, tennis, evenings
> at home; to build a long-term relationship.

Gabe chose to run his ad in a local suburban newspaper because he figured he'd then find someone who lived nearby. And he suspected that a larger percentage of professionals read the suburban paper than his local urban paper. His results? He got just one response. But the person who responded was just who he was seeking. When we last spoke with him, he was betting that they would become good friends.

The Language of Love

In any medium, words are important—even when pictures are involved. How you use them will determine your success. Jenny discovered this when she placed an ad back in 1985. While she didn't keep her ad, she remembers it was way too intimate to generate the sort of responses that she had hoped to attract. It went something like this:

> SWF, 23, decadent, free spirit. Enjoys
> bubble baths with champagne and strawberries.
> Looking for SWM with same interests.

Jenny received approximately 100 responses. Most were from older men. Many sent photos of themselves posing in front of their cars. One response was a picture of a guy with a huge beer gut holding a bottle of Mr. Clean and a bottle of Mr. Bubble who captioned the photo, "Mr. Clean makes getting clean as fun as getting dirty." While this may have been a clever response, it clearly wasn't the polished, romantic reply Jenny was seeking.

In retrospect, she realized that she was asking for trouble when she used the words *decadent* and *bubble baths* in the same ad. She just wanted to show her fun side and her stay-at-home quiet side. "It left me depressed," Jenny said of the results. This mistake taught Jenny the importance of her words. She hadn't realized how easily her ad could be misunderstood.

Like Jenny, Bruce, a 39-year-old Presbyterian minister, learned the importance of word implications. He placed an ad stating that he was a minister and only received a few responses—and most of those came from women who were incompatible with his liberal, adventurous nature. He then decided to hold off giving this information in his ad and reveal his occupation during the first phone conversation, but when he tried this tactic, many of the respondents lost interest. In his next ad, he described himself as spiritual, but that didn't work either. Some of the women who responded were born-again Christians (he found them too conservative) and one woman was into witchcraft. This showed him that he needed to be even more conscious of the connotations when describing his occupation and added the word "counselor" to his job description. He now seems to receive responses from women who can accept his role as a minister and still maintain the ability to have fun.

The bottom line: when compiling your list of words, be careful that, together they don't create a different meaning or have a nuance that you didn't intend to convey.

How Headlines Help

Why does your personal ad need a good headline? Because it's the best way to attract attention and help the reader focus on your message. At best a good headline should draw readers into the ad. It should tease them into wanting to know more. At the very least a headline should communicate the gist of the ad, so the reader has some idea of who you are. Then, if the reader chooses to move on to the next ad, he or she probably wasn't the person for you anyway.

For an example of a headline that helps indicate the writer's personality, take Dick's ad. He's a divorced, college-educated former zookeeper and office manager, who started using the personals because he didn't like picking up women in bars. For his ad, he wrote a headline that clearly spoke to its target group (women who saw themselves as being children of the '60s):

> Former hippie musician/activist seeks flower child. Nice-looking, romantic, kind DWM, 44 5'8", ISO S/DWF, 35–47, average height, weight, and looks, for equal, noncompetitive relationship. Smokers OK.

Dick chose his strategy of targeting flower children after a previous ad he'd run had generated more than 50 responses—with most of them coming from professional, career-oriented woman. He felt he'd wasted his time, hope, and energy, as well as the time, hope, and energy of all the women who had responded. With this new ad, he didn't receive as many responses—just six letters in all—but two of them came from women he now considers as possible partners in a long-term relationship.

For another example, see Valerie's ad in Chapter 2. She applied the same strategy with her headline, "Bulls, Bears, Beer." Separately each of those words don't mean too much. Many people are Bulls and Bears fans. Even more enjoy a good beer. But together, her headline screams "sports bar," which suggests a certain culture. Or take this ad, which ran in a Chicago-area newspaper:

> This is a numbers game and mine is worth calling. Blond, attractive, WJF, 5'8", young 45. Bright, master's, fun, very nice. Finding dates is easy, but seeking WM (Prof), 44–55ish, compatible, really good guy for "forever."

Who could resist the wordplay—and the attitude that wordplay conveys? The words clearly draw readers into the ad, making people want to read more. They also show that the writer of this ad is realistic about the dating scene and has a good level of self-esteem.

There are a few tricks that can help you get the best headline. First, just generate tons of them. Go for volume. Just churn out a huge pile of lines. Write as many as 30 different variations on the same concept. Then try different ideas. Play up all the different aspects of your personality—or the personality of your potential partner. By generating lots of different ideas, you can discover new possibilities. This helps you move past the easy solutions and loosens up your mind.

Then consider running with your first idea. We know. We just told you to generate lots of ideas. But for many people, their first idea is usually their best one—if they fully understand who they are, who they're trying to reach, and what type of relationship they want. If you don't use your first or early ideas, at least let them serve as a guide, giving you direction for the content of your ad.

Also, throughout the headline-writing process, you should remember to hone in on your target—not just to limit the number of responses that you'll get, but to increase their quality. That way you won't be overwhelmed by the sheer number of messages that you would have to wade through. Here are three flexible and clever strategies. The first will help you target your audience if you have conflicting interests. The second will help you quickly communicate your personality in your headline, as well as through the rest of the ad. And the third strategy could help you show how you can bring a missing ingredient and fit into the life of your special someone.

Other strategies—those that are used more often in traditional advertising—can be found in books on ad copywriting. Two good places to start: *The Copywriter's Handbook* by Robert Bly (he even includes a list of 32 ad concepts you can use) and *The Copy Workshop Workbook* by Bruce Bendinger.

Put Your Worst Foot Forward

Identify your roadblock to forming a successful relationship and use it to find your perfect mate. Perhaps you're filled with contradictory interests or you're fiercely independent. You may be the Christian who loves a wild party. The musician with a stable income. A health nut who enjoys an occasional dinner out at Bob's Bar-B-Q & Steak O'Rama. Maybe you have a physical disability. If so, you've probably learned that people use stereotypes to judge you. People often attribute additional qualities to you that you may or may not possess. Admit it. We all do it.

Our strategy: creatively play up the negative. Address the roadblock directly. Why? Because it will help screen out people who aren't right for you as well as possibly attract people who are perfect for you. Mark in Chapter 3 used this strategy when he wrote in his computer profile that he is HIV positive—and as you may recall, the response he got was great.

Cindy also found this strategy to be successful. A very attractive, energetic woman, she felt that it was hopeless to find *one* person with the qualities that were most important to her. At 36, she was living in her newly rehabbed downtown loft, enjoying her friends, and every few months, meeting someone worth dating. The trouble was, she was ready to settle down. Yet she never found her two passions—art and sports—in the same man. She wanted a man who'd attend a wine-and-cheese gallery opening on Friday evening and go in-line skating on Saturday afternoon. She had traditional Christian values that she wanted her mate to share, but she found that many men who shared those values disapproved of her appreciation for chocolate martinis. To make finding a mate even more difficult, she had high standards in the looks department. Her friends told her she was being too picky.

But then one friend urged Cindy to place a personal ad and ask for the most difficult-to-find qualities right up front. "Then if a guy continues reading the ad," her friend said, "at least he's the sort of guy who might interest you." Cindy took this advice and wrote this ad:

Renoir to Rollerblading . . .
Downtown, athletic, graphic designer, SWF, 36, 5′10″ with high energy, Christian values, seeking fit, attractive, humorous, intelligent S/DWM, 32–42, to enjoy museums, theater, summer art shows, biking, tennis, skiing, & flirting with possibility of long-term relationship. No drugs, cats, or smoking.

Her headline referenced art and sports in a specific but fun way that demonstrated her interests to her readers. The body copy identified her other qualities and indicated the type of relationship she was seeking, as well as some qualities that she wanted to avoid in a mate.

Cindy received about 15 responses. Most of them were from men who seemed nice enough, but some were in the process of divorce, which she felt wouldn't lead to one of them offering an engagement ring in the near future. Several were above her acceptable age range. One man she met for dinner was extremely boring. Another was good-looking, fun, and interesting—just the type she was seeking—but after a few more dates, she began to suspect that he was economically unstable and then she realized that they weren't quite on the same wavelength.

With her voice-mail number almost ready to expire, Cindy concluded that, while she hadn't met Mr. Right, there were nice men out there and that maybe finding a mate wasn't so hopeless after all . . . and there was one more number in her voice mailbox that she hadn't called back yet.

Brad was a divorced physicist who enjoyed art, sports, and church—he was even great looking! Cindy was thrilled. She met him for a drink and they clicked. That was a few months ago; at this writing, they're still dating—and even talking about marriage.

Try a Simile or a Metaphor

Another powerful targeting technique is to let readers know more about you by using a metaphor or simile in your headline (as well as body copy). It works for many reasons. It's more entertaining than reading the tired old lines like, "enjoy sailing, bowling, outdoors, long talks . . ." (you can fill in the rest); it gives readers something to play with; and it opens the door for them to respond creatively with a simile or metaphor of their own. Best of all, when you choose a comparison that's right for you, it does actually communicate. For example: Casey's sister met her spouse through personal ads, so Casey thought maybe the personals could work for him, too. "Most people my age go to bars to meet people," he said, "but even at 26, I'm getting sick of it." Casey wanted a different theme, so he picked fruits and vegetables.

What Fruit or Vegetable Do You Resemble?
I'm like garlic . . . sound strange? Well, I have a very aggressive, extroverted personality with flamboyant presentation (attractive). Looking for sexy fruit (female) for a little nosh. SJM, 26, 6'0", 190. Weight reasonably proportioned to height, please.

The results? He got about five responses, most referencing a fruit of some sort. One came from a Russian immigrant. Another was from a very attractive social worker. He noted that some of the respondents looked good on paper but didn't quite measure up. Generally, however, he was pleased with his experiences dating through the personals.

"I'm always surprised that most of the respondents are really nice, hip people," he said. "The perception that only losers write and respond to ads is wrong."

Creating an effective personal ad like Casey's by using a simile or metaphor is easier than you may think. In Chapters 3 and 4, you came up with adjectives that described yourself and your ideal partner. Now, through brainstorming, simply give those words a twist and generate creative concepts—or the overall idea behind your ad. This will give you a framework to help make your ad stand apart from the rest. Look at the words that you had previously identified and let them inspire you. Let's say you described yourself as being musical. What instrument do you resemble? If you like wild animals, which one would you choose to be? Are you like a color? A game? A city? A flower? Then compare yourself to the item. It's that easy!

When creating an ad with a simile or metaphor (or with some other creative twist), it's best to let ideas hit you immediately. Don't edit. Rather, give yourself permission to generate bad ideas and headlines and to use bland language. Open-minded, free thinking allows some bad ideas to come along, but good ideas will come, too.

Once you hit on the idea that you want to pursue, you can refine your words to improve the headlines as well as the body copy. How do you know when you've hit on the right idea? Bruce Bendinger, in his book *The Copy Workshop Workbook,* provides four questions by which to judge an idea. With questions geared toward advertising students and professionals, he suggests that one ask:

1. Is it faithful to the strategy?
2. Does it have genuine substance?
3. Is it credible yet challenging?
4. Is it provocative?

If you can say yes to each of the questions, then you have a strong concept.

Tell a Story

Like fairy tales? Tell a story that presents your fantasy. Enjoy fishing? Make up a story about fishing and weave in your specifics. Create—or bring to life a conflict—and show how a date or relationship with you can solve it. Ellen, from Chapter 3, did this with her ad that started, "Hoping to meet a beautiful, young, wealthy, voluptuous, but thin, 'girl of his dreams,' he anxiously dials the mailbox number from a *Reader* matches ad." This draws the reader into the ad, because he could identify with the situation.

Bruce Bendinger, again in the *The Copy Workshop Workbook*, reminds readers that story ads were once very common but are now used less, especially in print advertising. There are all sorts of examples of story ads in consumer advertising that you can use as examples—everything from the classics like "Always a Bridesmaid, Never a Bride" for Listerine and "They All Laughed When I Sat Down at the Piano" to the campy ads for pimple cream and x-ray spec ads that you can find in the back of old comic books. For a more contemporary example, watch for the testimonial commercials you see broadcast on late-night or early-morning television, particularly on cable.

Romance and Dance with Your Body Copy

Once you've generated your headline, it's time to write your ad. You can start by using one of the rejected headlines as your first sentence and as your closing sentence. Remember, just like writing a headline, play with your words. Try different ways of saying the same thing. Have fun with it. Very few effective ads come out directly and make a statement. You're selling a good feeling about what it's like to be around you, so create a positive image. Remember that a stronger, better headline is often buried in your body copy, so keep your eyes open for it. Don't be afraid to change directions and use it. In addition, be sure to use the common abbreviations that have evolved for personal ads (listed in Appendix B), simply to help you save space and money. What's more, your ad should do the following.

Talk to Your Target One-on-One

Your ad will be most effective when it communicates directly to that one person you want to reach. So ignore the rest of the readership in the newspaper or magazine. You don't have to appeal to everyone. Just make it sing to that ideal version of the special someone and you should have success with the personals. In fact, if your headline has done its job fully, the entire readership of the magazine or newspaper probably would not be reading your ad—just your select few. And how should you talk to your target? Just as you would to any friend, new or old. Use simple, casual language—even fragments—and make it sound like you're having a conversation with someone. The less formal, the better. After all, who really wants to be in a long-term relationship with a stiff?

Convey an "Attitude"

Yes, we said that your ad must be informative. But it needs to be more than that. You don't just want to inform that special someone about yourself and the type of relationship you want—that could make you sound boring; rather, you need to form a bond with that person. And the best way to do that is by appealing to fear, security, joy, humor, love, romance, aspirations, and a long list of other human needs. So pay attention to the tone, voice, and attitude you convey in an ad. They have to be appropriate to your message.

Show, Don't Tell

Your ad should exhibit your qualities, not just recite them. If you have a sense of humor, be amusing. If you are intelligent, be smart. And if you are adventurous . . . well, you *are* placing a personal ad. It's easy to show your qualities when you convey a particular attitude. For example, remember Steve from Chapter 3? His ad didn't mention specifics about himself, but by showcasing his poetry and songwriting talents, he did reveal his attitude about life and values. And, he did get responses, with many of them coming from people who were clearly on his same wavelength. So remember, the more you put your personality into your ad, the more that special someone will want to meet you.

Indicate Your Levels of Interest

It's not enough to declare an interest in sports or reading. A man who coaches hockey has a different level of interest in that sport than someone who enjoys watching an occasional game on television, but both may say they love sports. Reading is another vague, overused term. Is he or she talking about reading two books a year off the bestseller list? The Sunday comics? A fashion magazine? Or the collected works of Franz Kafka—in German? What about a sense of humor? Would that be in the form of the Three Stooges? Comedy clubs? Practical jokes? Political satire? Or dry, dark, sarcastic quips? The point we're trying to make is that in your quest for cleverness, you don't want to lose sight of the facts. Make sure you're specific about all of your points, because this will make you more real to your readers. And that's what makes people want to get to know more about you.

Go Against the Grain

When you read the publication in which you want your ad to appear, study the tone of all the other personals. If you see them yelling, whisper. If you see the ads being filled with bad puns, use declarative sentences. If you see that they're all using creative twists, be more straightforward. Why? Because when you do the opposite of the other ads in the publication (or wherever you decide to place your ad), you'll stand out and get noticed. And if your someone special doesn't notice you, you've lost the battle.

Turn Negatives into Positives

In any personal ad, part of your task is to communicate your features and how they might benefit a potential partner. You need to do more than just describe yourself in a positive light. It's not enough to change an adjective like *fat* into *full-figured* or *bald* into *follicularly-challenged.* And it's not right to make people read between the lines. After all, effective ads honestly offer the reader something. If you have a demanding career that limits the time you can share with someone, ask for a "low-maintenance relationship." If you're a custodial parent of four children under 12, write "Missing Out on Legos and Lullabies?" The reader will respect your confidence, and if you've offered more appealing qualities as well, and if he or she is right for you, you'll get a call.

Proceed with Caution When Using Humor

Yes, this might sound like a slight contradiction from the previous suggestion, but we want you to be forewarned: humor often falls flat in print. Without the benefit of a good delivery, the effort is often wasted. People might not understand that you're trying to be funny. This becomes obvious during on-line conversations when humorous or sarcastic comments are mistaken for insults or flippant remarks. Even in traditional advertising, very few print ads are really hysterically funny. If you think you've got a funny ad, test it on a few friends just to make sure. After all, who wants to send the wrong message to Mr. or Ms. Right?

Make It Unique to You

Give readers an idea of your interests, beliefs, and lifestyle with a creative twist. As we said before, focus on word connotations. Create a natural feel. And convey a sense of fun. Create an emotional bond right from the beginning. The effectiveness of your ad is partially determined by the language you use. Don't ignore it. Rather, consider it while you write. Play with your word choices. Try to identify a unique tone for your ad; this is what creates an emotional feeling.

After placing a series of ads throughout the years, John learned to work hard to make his ad unique. His first ad was placed in 1985, when he was living in Virginia. He was new in town and didn't know anyone. The local paper held a contest for the ad of the week. The winning ad was featured and was run for free. John's ad won because it was funny. Since he'd just gotten out of graduate school, he decided to use the headline "Recently Released Male." The result: no responses. So he went back to his old method of meeting women through singles events for graduates and Catholics.

When he relocated to Chicago, he tried the personals again. This time he went for a more straightforward approach and wrote something like:

> SWM, 32, 180, 6 foot, likes movies, theater, and fine dining, seeks single female, 25–35.

He placed the ad in the *Tribune,* as well as the *Reader,* and got a total of nine responses—one from the *Tribune* and eight from the *Reader.* He got back to all of them, met three of them, and dated one for a couple of months. But they broke up because they didn't have much in common.

He tried the personals again a few months later, using the same ad, but putting in more about himself: that he had an advanced degree and that he liked blues and jazz. Then in his voice-mail message, he told even more about himself as well as thanked the woman for calling. His results? He again received nine response—this time, from just one placement instead of two—but a greater percentage of the respondents were well educated and held advanced degrees. He called all of them back and met six of them for coffee.

"I started to meet women who shared the same interests and background," he said. Since none of these dates turned into a long-term romance, he tried the personals again, this time putting even more of himself into the ad by giving more details. He wrote:

> SWM, dark blond, brown eyes, 33, 6′ tall, 180 lbs, educated, degreed, likes blues, jazz, and fine dining seeks single female, 25–35, who enjoys moonlight sailing and a nice guy.

Again the quality of his responses improved and he started dating a woman who was working on her Ph.D. They broke up, however, because she was looking for a long-term future and he just wanted to have fun. When a friend saw the results he was getting, he convinced John to write with him:

> Two single guys—a professional and a
> carpenter—looking for sailing companions.

This was a disaster. They got four replies and met with two of them. They were all older—slightly above 35—and John and his friend found none of them attractive. "Different people read different ads," said John. "Since there was less risk with a couples ad, we tended to meet women who were rejected a lot." Although he never stated a weight requirement in his ads for himself, most of the women he met were physically fit. So he went back to placing an ad for himself. This time he wanted to say even more about his personality and sense of humor and crafted the following ad:

> SWM, 34, Jeep owner: Good condition, rugged, well
> built, quiet runner, very reliable, adaptable, all-terrain vehicle.
> Should last a lifetime with proper maintenance and TLC.
> Seeks female companion, 25–35. Make or model unimportant.
> Small to midsize, sharp, with quick response, able to handle
> well in all conditions. Call today for a test drive.

This time he received seven responses, met all of them at a coffee shop (one at a time, of course), went on dates with four of them, and dated three of them more than once. And he started dating Marcia more than the rest. Within several months, he was dating her exclusively. They eventually moved in together and then, approximately three years after meeting, they got married.

John found that all of the women who answered this ad were more creative—and all had at least a master's degree. "I just got more of myself into the ad," he said, explaining his results. "The woman who read and enjoyed my ad already enjoyed my sense of humor or wit, so we already had a more personal connection from the start."

So what was his method for writing this final ad? "I just sat down at my computer and listed the things I enjoyed," he explained. "I owned a Jeep and came up with that as a metaphor for myself. It fit well with me: I'm a carpenter and I dress in flannel and jeans."

John isn't the only one to discover that a unique description of himself could help him meet quality people. Cindy, 44, also used this strategy. Returning to the singles scene after 25 years of marriage and raising one son and three stepchildren, she at first tried a dating service, but her only memorable date from that endeavor was with a man who had a shoe fetish. Cindy then decided to try the personals. She felt that this would give her an opportunity to get to know a prospect before wasting time on a date. And it helped her meet more men, more quickly than the dating service. She placed the following ad in her local paper, which was in a town of about 100,000 people just south of Denver:

> Antique teenager, secure professional enjoys theater, music, cats, travel, broncos, avalanches, Rockies, computer and lifelong learning seeks outgoing NS, SM 40 to 55.

Since her first ad, she has placed four ads in four years. Her varied interests have attracted a wide variety of men, including a smoker, someone significantly shorter than she, a married man who wanted dates for the theater, and a chauvinist. She discovered that because of her long list of interests (a roadblock that could have also been used to help her better target her ideal man), most men just picked up on one or two of the items listed in her ad and ignored the rest. However, she has been able to develop two friendships—one of which she describes as "very close"— and she continues to use the personals for finding dates. Her motto when writing ads: "Age and treachery will overcome youth and skill."

Create an Emotional Bond

Facts inform. Emotions motivate. So establishing an emotional connection is what makes an ad successful. If you're entertaining, funny, sarcastic, irreverent, and smart, use those qualities in your ad. This is what gives it some punch. Surprise your readers. Inspire them. Show them that you're a human being. Make readers feel that they would enjoy being around you. Your feelings will be relevant to that special someone—which is why so many people we interviewed told us that they responded to others who struck them as *sincere* as much as to the explicit content of the ad or response. When you strike an essential truth, you will receive responses from those who relate to you.

Use Language That Reflects You

Your ad should sound like you sound in everyday life. Then it will have a truthful, special quality, giving it credibility. If you have a casual style, use a casual approach. Even use sentence fragments. The less formal, the better. You'll seem approachable and friendly. And if you're a university professor who's most comfortable with polysyllabic words, use them. Be aware that the more away from the norm your ad, the more you limit the *quantity* of responses. Even if a reader understands the words you use, he or she may think you're being pompous or arrogant for using them in a personal ad. Those same words may, however, help you reach the person of your dreams, someone who uses polysyllabic words too.

Include a Call to Action

Outside of image advertising that is designed to build awareness for a brand's personality, most successful advertising invites the reader to take the next step—whether that's to call an 800-number, visit a website, return a response card, visit a store, or try a product. You too can increase the likelihood of a response if you sign off with such an invitation. In fact, a line like "So call already," "Just do it," or "I'd love to talk with you" can actually be the clincher in motivating someone to respond. It's just like a sales representative asking for the sale. There's nothing wrong with doing this—if it's done in an inviting, friendly, nonthreatening way.

Let Your Ad Evolve

So what makes the perfect personal ad? Whatever works for you. Every good personal ad is unique. Communicating your character— what's unique about you or your unique selling proposition—is what gives the reader a reason to be interested in you and to respond. Identifying who you want to meet and the type of relationship you want is what tells the reader whether you'd be interested in meeting him or her. That's all there is to it.

When George started using the personals, he learned this the hard way. He ran an ad that didn't work. Recently divorced, he just wanted social relationships, so he decided to try a promotional ad. It read:

> GRAB YOUR BIKINI; WE'RE OFF TO CANCUN!
> Looking for short, educated, sexy woman, 28+,
> comfortable in black tie or jeans for trip to sunny
> beach. Me? Business owner, successful author,
> MBA, loves fine dining and travel, good looking,
> sense of humor, own hair, 5'7", 48.

The results? George got a couple of responses from women looking for companionship and a vacation. "Who wants to be a winner of a contest?" George asked in retrospect. "People are generally serious about dating. And I didn't reveal much about myself." So he decided to try again with a totally new ad. And it was more successful. From then on, he started refining his ads. His strategy was to differentiate himself from the other guys—through honesty. "Lies backfire. I didn't want to get caught in that situation," he said. "I wonder why you would lie at something so obvious." So what did his final ad look like? Here it is:

> ANY WOMAN OUT THERE with brains and beauty?
> Smart, educated, and sexy dresser? Opinionated,
> accomplished, and a body made for Versace and La Perla?
> Me? Successful business owner, published writer, MBA,
> refreshingly honest, English, curious, fairly handsome, 5'7",
> youthful 50. Enjoys tennis, politics, newspapers, storefront
> theater, talk shows, modern dance. Possible LTR.

As you can see, this ad is longer than his first one, but it also explains more about George and the type of person he is seeking. His results? "I got higher-quality responses," he said. In all, he placed a total of six ads. And he found it to be a worthwhile experience. Dating through the personals enabled him to better define the type of relationship he wanted as well as the type of woman he wanted to meet. And based on these experiences, he found his way to a long-term relationship with an advertising executive. Of his success, he said, "I just picked out what defined me—such as owning a business—and women were able to develop an image of me in their heads."

Media-Specific Creative and Production Tips

Throughout all media, your idea or concept has to be sound—and a strong idea will translate —or pool out—from one medium to another. But in many cases, the medium that you choose will help drive the form and content of your message. So if you're using a nontraditional medium for personal ads, read through the pertinent points provided below. These suggestions work in tandem with the idea provided in the last chapter, which covered many of the advantages and disadvantages of different mediums. Here, you'll find tips to help you maximize the creative impact within those considerations. Please note that some of the tips such as those in the video section will also help you get the most out of dating services, and other pointers will also help if you reply to an ad.

Space Advertising

What's the difference between a print classified ad and a space ad? Well, here you can—and should—think visually. Let your picture, in conjunction with your headline, do most of the work. The body copy becomes secondary. Use the combination of the headline and picture to dramatize your unique selling proposition.

For ideas on laying out your ad, just look at your favorite magazines. But as David Herzbrum advises in his book for beginning professional copywriters called *Copywriting by Design,* one shouldn't try to be a designer. Instead, use a standard layout; then let your ideas emerge and your layout should evolve from there. You need to avoid long sentences as well as long gray blocks of copy. Instead, cut out as many words as possible and shorten paragraphs. Use subheads to guide your readers through your ad.

As for producing the ad, talk to the publication in which you want it to run. Since the publication wants to earn the money for the space, the ad manager may help arrange for you to use one of the staff designers, but keep in mind that many of these designers have more experience in laying out running text than ads. In giving direction to them, let them know that your ad shouldn't be too slick. The more authentic and homespun, the better. And include a line letting people know that your ad is *not* one for a dating service; otherwise, there may be confusion among readers, leading people to disregard your ad.

Billboard or Bulletin Board Advertising

In the previous chapter we showed how some polished outdoor board presentations led to misunderstanding and confusion among the audience. Such billboards can make people think they are looking at a sign for a dating service or—worse—a joke. Don't let this happen to you. Your outdoor or bulletin board ad shouldn't be too slick. Rather, you should aim to make it more straightforward, even handmade and perhaps amateurish, with hand-printed lettering.

Meanwhile, since there's very little time to read an outdoor board as well as figure out that it's actually a personal ad, you should also make sure your design is very clean. The creative concept probably can be taken from your print ad and then simplified. If you can use a picture, do so. This will make your ad even more approachable and readable.

To get information on producing an outdoor board—one that isn't handwritten—contact the Outdoor Advertising Institute. And since most boards are rented from large companies, the owner of the particular billboard you want to rent should help you in locating a graphic designer to produce your artwork. But in judging this work, there are a few things you should insist upon.

- Make the print large enough to read at a distance.
- Keep it short. Less than seven words is ideal.
- Make sure there's contrast between the words and the background. Blue letters on a black background may seem dramatic and interesting, but make sure the print is legible.

On-Line Advertising

Dating through on-line personals is a booming market. And each service provider has its own specifications. Some allow you to include photographs while others don't. Some are also a little better about keeping your anonymity. So be sure to check them out thoroughly before deciding which one to use. In the meantime, here are a few creative guidelines to get you going.

- Although the unlimited space may tempt you to write several pages of copy, try instead to be concise. After all, you don't want to overwhelm your readers.
- Proofread your words and, although you want your copy to sound conversational, follow the principles of good grammar. After all, you don't want people to think that you don't know what you're doing—or that you are uneducated.
- Treat file subjects or titles like a headline, but use shorthand so you can include your age, sex, and sexual preference: 28 yo SHM 4 SF 4 Big "M." (For more on abbreviations and shorthand, see Appendix B.)
- Use smileys (or emoticons, as they are more commonly called)—letters typed together to form pictures. These symbols are well recognized—and used—within the computing community. So using them in your ad could help give you copy some personality and lend shading to your words. (For more on this, see Appendix B.)
- Put a Web page together. But say something more than "I'm available." Otherwise you may look perpetually unattached, a person whose longest relationships are perhaps no longer than a Thanksgiving weekend. If you put together a website, you can then reference it in a more traditional Internet personal ad environment.

Audio Advertising

Anyone who leaves a message on an answering machine is, in essence, creating a radio spot. But unlike commercial radio, you don't want to sound too slick. As we said earlier, we found that people look for sincerity and authenticity and they use the sound of the voice as their biggest indicator. George learned this over the course of the ads that he had placed. He knew that the voice-mail section was a place for him to go into more detail about himself. So at first he scripted out his messages. Here's the voice-mail message that went along with his first ad:

Hi, my name is George. I'm looking for a woman who'd enjoy a long weekend in Cancun. Someone who likes fine dining, movies, concerts, and an occasional museum.

I'm looking for a special person. A professional woman. Is equally comfortable in a short skirt and an evening gown. Someone who is smart, self-confident, and a good conversationalist.

I'm 48, own a business, and am professionally secure. Friends tell me I'm not bad looking, have a great sense of humor, and am pretty down to earth.

I'd like to hear from you. Leave your name and phone number and describe yourself and I'll get back to you. Thanks for calling.

When George decided to try the personals again, he completely rewrote his voice-mail message. Here's what he recorded for his second ad:

Hi. My name is George. You know what I'm looking for. Let me tell you about me. I'm 48, five-foot-seven, trim, pretty good looking. I play racquetball and tennis regularly.

I was born in England, although I don't have much of an accent left. Have an MBA, own my own business, and, financially, I'm doing pretty well.

I don't care much for football or baseball. But I love a great conversation. I really like smart, well-dressed women. Women with an opinion and not afraid of stating it. I enjoy going to the latest restaurants, foreign films, and beaches in the Caribbean. Friends say I have a good sense of humor, and I read everything from the New York Times *to the* National Enquirer.

If you think we have a few things in common, I'd love to talk to you.

As you can see from George's two examples, there was less wordplay and he was more himself during the second message. He was also less rehearsed and more personal. In his later message, he became even more relaxed about the process. If he forgot to say something, he'd just interject it when he remembered it. His goal was to sound more human and credible—and it worked. Why did he write everything out initially? Because recording a greeting can be intimidating at first. Once he got comfortable with the system, he wasn't intimidated by it. To help you get over the intimidation factor while helping your announcement stand out, here is some additional advice.

- If you have music in the background, it should stay in the background and not conflict with your voice. You want people to be able to hear and understand everything you say.
- Speak much slower than you normally would speak when recording a message, enabling a listener to understand and process all of the information you provide without having to go back to the beginning. Remember, unlike the print medium, the listener can't easily go back to the beginning to see if he or she missed something.
- Use a stopwatch to time your announcement to make sure that it isn't too long. Even if your voice-mail supplier doesn't limit your time speaking, people are getting accustomed to shorter and shorter radio spots. If you leave too long a message, people will tune out.

Video Advertising

Prime-time network television wasn't what you had in mind when you decided to place a personal ad, so why are video tips relevant? There are several reasons: First, you could exchange videos by mail. Second, it's now possible to send short clips over the Internet and in the near future this could become very common. Third, if you hire a dating service, they may want to tape you. And, finally, you never know when a personal-ads television program will pop up. Most of the advice given in the audio section holds here; in addition, you may want to keep the following tips in mind.

- Think visually. Like a space ad, find images and pictures that can help bring to life your unique selling proposition.
- Rehearse in front of a mirror until you feel comfortable and confident.
- Know what you want to say and speak naturally. Don't read your copy.
- Wear bright colors, but stay away from white and patterns.
- Keep it short. People will decide very quickly if they want to meet you or not—probably within 15 seconds.

Edit at the End

You've got your ad ready. It's neatly typed. There are no typos. You're almost ready to go. You may wish to show it to a friend or two. Get their input. As we saw with Jenny's bubble bath ad, you may think that your ad says one thing, but others may interpret it differently. So seek advice. Showing your ad to others will keep you from frustrating yourself by presenting a concept that's unclear or that has an unintentional double meaning. But beyond that, there's no easy way to tell a good idea from a bad one—unless it works. There are, however, criteria that can help keep you from making blatant mistakes, which we have converted into the handy checklist below. Eventually you may wish to develop your own questions based on the ads that have generated the types of responses you're seeking as well as your experiences with your local dating scene. With our checklist, the more questions to which you can answer yes, the better off you are.

1. Is everything spelled and punctuated correctly with correct grammar usage?
2. Is the headline relevant to your personality?
3. Does it indicate what type of relationship you want?
4. Does it target the type of person you'd like to meet?
5. Is it the kind of idea—and does it have the content—that's unique to you?
6. Is it motivating and persuasive?
7. Is it entertaining, enabling you to attract somebody's attention?

8. Does it ask readers to participate in the ad?
9. Do you like it? And does it bring a smile to your face?
10. Do you get a tiny tingling in your stomach? Does it make you a little nervous?
11. Does it sound conversational?
12. Is it as specific as you can be about yourself?
13. Is this ad about someone you'd want to get to know?
14. Does it include a call to action?

Say What?

Thought is the blossom; language the bud; action the fruit behind it.

—Ralph Waldo Emerson

The following situation is typical: you are relaxing in your favorite chair or at your favorite coffee shop and reading your local newspaper when you find your way to the personals section. Some of the ads amuse you. Others repulse you. A few intrigue you. But there's one that almost—but not quite—gets you to pick up the phone. You may begin to wonder, "What would happen if I did respond? What do I have to lose?" You hesitate at first. Then you pick up the phone. And before you realize it, you've discovered the benefits of dating through the personals.

For many people, responding to an ad is the first step into the exciting world of dating through the personals. They find they feel more comfortable in this role. And they discover that they're able to meet interesting people by responding. They may want to form friendships and love relationships; they may even seek to meet their long-term partners and future spouses. After all, for personal ads to work, someone has to be the respondent.

In many ways, responding to an ad is just like placing one. But in other ways it's very different: when you place an ad, no one has any idea who you are or where you live. All you have to do is sit back and wait for the letters or the voice-mail messages to arrive. But responding can be risky business. You have to work through all those confusing voice-mail commands you need to follow. You have to explain why you fit someone's requirements. You have to open yourself up and leave a name and number. Sending in a response is like applying for a job. You don't know who'll be seeing it or how many people will be competing against you for a date.

But like applying for a job that's a fit with your interests and abilities, responding to a personal ad is also empowering. You get to select from all of the ads. And you can take control of your dating life by making sure you get introduced to the type of person you want to meet. What's more, your results are inherently more immediate.

This chapter will show you some tips that can make responding easier and help you get better results. Plus, it will give you an idea of what to expect and what to say. To help you get the most out of this chapter, however, you should have also worked through the exercises in Chapters 2 through 4. The points you identified in those chapters can help you identify the people you want to meet as well as craft your response. But assuming that you've read and completed all of the exercises, let's begin. After all, what do you have to lose?

Make a Date to Start

If responding to a personal ad intimidates you, get your feet wet first. How? By listening to voice-mail messages. You don't have to respond. Listen to both men and women. This will give you a feel for the voices behind the ads and hear your competition. As we mentioned in Chapter 4, when Shawn became interested in answering the personals, he spent time listening to a variety of voice-mail ads. This process gave him the confidence to respond. And it could help make you comfortable with responding as well. So even though this might cost some money, it'll help you when you finally do respond to an ad.

You don't even have to select a particular ad. Most voice-mail systems allow you to move from one message to another without entering a particular phone number. Of course, this method will allow you to browse through the ads on the system but will not allow you to target people with specific attributes or interests.

Sally, whom we first met in Chapter 1, likes to answer ads. She first reads the newspaper, finding the ads that interest her. Then she listens to their voice-mail messages, cutting down the possibilities. Finally, when a message interests her, she leaves a response.

If you find a message that interests you when you're doing your test, you may just want to jump in and leave a response. But there are a few important points to keep in mind.

When an advertiser writes an ad, he or she has to be very choosy about what to say. If the advertiser sounds like the woman of your dreams, but she wants a nonsmoker—and you're not one—move on. If a man's ad describes you perfectly, except he wants a slim woman and you're battling the scale, move on. If a woman says she's looking for a possible marriage, but you know it will be a decade before you'd be interested in tying the knot, move on. The biggest complaint that we got from people who'd placed personal ads was that they received numerous responses from people who ignored points covered in the ad. They automatically rejected these respondents—either in this stage if they could tell that the attributes didn't match their expectations or after the first meeting (when it's harder to hide personal attributes). So there's no use wasting your time and energy on someone who probably wouldn't want to be with you—even if you did get one date out of the deal.

If you're not sure whether you should respond when some of your qualities don't match with a particular quality that the advertiser is seeking, consider the emphasis the ad places on it; the degree to which you vary; and its importance to the relationship. For example, an advertiser whose headline states "Tennis Partner Wanted" is placing far more emphasis on finding someone interested in tennis than an ad that simply mentions tennis as one of the interests in the body copy. If you're not into tennis, you could consider responding to the ad that mentions the person's casual interest in the game but not to the one seeking a partner for the game.

Also, weigh the degree to which you vary from the advertiser's specifications. The ad may present an age range of 35 to 55. If you're a few years younger or older, it shouldn't matter. But if, for example, the age range is between 35 and 42 and you're 49, it may be too much of a difference. The same is true for qualities such as weight, height, traveling distance, and other characteristics that are described in the ad.

Likewise, consider how important the item is to a relationship. If an advertiser appears to have all the qualities you could ever want, but says no to previous marriages and children and you're divorced with four children, forget it. Maybe he or she wants a nonsmoker. Or someone to share a country lifestyle. These are critical items that you would need to come to terms with as a couple, and plenty of couples do, but why look for trouble when so many ads present fewer conflicts?

You should also be sensitive to the terms in an ad. You may see terms like *free spirit, discreet,* or *full-figured.* What do these really mean? The person who describes himself or herself as a free spirit may not be interested in settling down. *Discreet* can imply that someone is married or has a significant other and clearly isn't a prospect who will take you to his or her office Christmas party or family reunion. And, there are many euphemisms for overweight, including *Rubenesque, full-figured, king-* or *queen-sized,* or *stocky.* So you must read between the lines and look at the spirit of the ad as well as the explicit words. Take a close look at each word in the ad and if you're not sure what the advertiser means, ask for clarification in your response.

Asking a question also gives the advertiser a good reason to call you back. If, while talking, you discover something about him or her that's unappealing you can say something like, "That's not something I'm looking for in a person." No big deal. It just wasn't a match.

Finally, while combing the personals, keep an open mind (without lowering your standards). Just like people who write an ad, identify your must-haves. Then, with each ad, ask yourself, "Does it respond appropriately to my needs?" For instance, are you settling for a smoker, because she seduced you with exquisite measurements? Don't do it! What seems tolerable in the beginning is likely to evolve into a major issue. That's why it's wise to decide ahead of time exactly what qualities are important to you, as well as what nice surprises you're willing to accept.

Think Through Your Response

Today, most personal-ad responses are received through telephone voice response systems, but some publications still offer mailboxes for letters. These methods require different considerations. For instance, with either method, it's important to tell the advertiser why you chose to respond to his or her ad. But you can't do it the same way. Sarah discovered this when she decided to reply to an ad placed by Victor, a 32-year old cartoonist. She came up with this cartoon response (with which she included her name and telephone number):

Her cartoon not only provided some information on herself, it was something a cartoonist would easily be able to relate to. And he did. As a matter of fact, he told her it was his favorite response. They had an entertaining lunch filled with laughter, but because they seemed to be in different places in life, neither one followed up. But, obviously, Sarah could not have responded the same way if Victor had asked for a voice-mail response. She would have had to find some other way to connect with him.

As Sarah's experience shows, there are many decisions that you have to make when you respond to an ad. Should you be suggestive? Flirtatious? Straightforward? Humorous? What phone number should you leave? When should you tell the person to call? Should you come on strong? The answer is simple. Use your best judgment—your intuition. You're the best one to judge the situation, the advertiser's attitude, and your own comfort level.

But to help you develop your intuition, we'll address both methods of responding. We will cover voice-mail responses first and then written responses (which cover on-line personals). Be sure to combine this information with what you learn in Chapter 9 on security before you respond to any particular ad. This will help you to be not only successful, but safe.

Voice-Mail Responses

The more popular—and more expensive—way to reply, the voice-mail response is also your most immediate. You can leave a response and within hours or perhaps even minutes hear back from the person. Here are some success secrets for using voice mail.

Listen to the Voice. For some people, this is a very important part of the attraction. For others, it's more important to see the face behind the voice. Either way, a voice can tell you something about a person's other qualities. For instance, it can indicate a reassuring, confident, insecure, or hurried demeanor. Grammar and diction often are clues to the individual's educational level. Tone can indicate a serious or playful personality. But keep in mind that one's voice does not indicate one's appearance. There are professional voice-over artists and disc jockeys who have extremely seductive, polished, and rich voices but are not very physically attractive. Likewise, there are many attractive people who have odd voices or are somewhat inarticulate. So if you find that an advertiser's voice is the only unappealing element, give yourself the opportunity to learn more about that individual because, just as we can grow to find qualities that we initially thought endearing to be irritating, sometimes we can come to appreciate traits that we first thought were negative.

Listen to the Complete Message. Just as you need to pay attention to the words in an ad, you need to listen to the content in the voice message. Often the voice message provides you with more detailed information than the ad. Also listen for a comment or reference to something that will open the door to a clever response. And try to gauge how natural and sincere the individual comes across. The way the message is crafted can be an indication of the advertiser's outlook or personality. Also, listen to see if there are any time limitations for your response. Telecommunications companies vary in the amount of response time they allow. So make sure your response fits into the allotted time.

Hang Up. When you call an advertiser, it's easy to pay more attention to the voice in your head that's wondering how—and if—you should leave a response, rather than to the voice or the content in the message. For this reason, your response may be more effective if you first listen closely to the tape and then simply hang up. This will give you a chance to process the information and call back after formulating your response.

Don't Put All Your Eggs in One Basket. Choose several ads that interest you. That way, you have a better chance of hearing from someone and you're not relying so heavily on the outcome of any particular advertiser, so you'll sound more carefree. This will show in your attitude and help you to sound less self-conscious and therefore more attractive.

Get Organized. To respond to more than one ad, you need to keep track of the message that you left. On a note pad, jot down the date, publication, as well as key words from the ad. (See Appendix D for our suggested form.) Then when you listen to the voice greeting, write down the individual's name and any additional information that will help you recognize one advertiser from another. You should also save your notes because if you use the personals regularly, you could very well leave a second response with the same advertiser, which could be embarrassing.

Address the Critical Issues. In the first half of this book, you learned that a good ad should describe you, your ideal partner, and the kind of relationship you want. Your response should do the same. It's also a good idea to acknowledge some of the interests you have in common with the advertiser. And you can encourage further dialogue by asking questions about information provided in the ad. Examples include: "So, what kind of wine should I have waiting for you by the fireplace?" "I'm taking a ballroom dance class. What kind of dancing are you referring to?" or "How many times did you actually parachute out of a plane?" This gives the advertiser something to talk about when returning your message.

Be Positive. You only have a few minutes to make a good impression, so don't use that time whining about your divorce or how difficult it is to meet nice people. One advertiser told us that she didn't like to read ads that say to "respond if you're not the sort of person who places or responds to these ads." Her comment: "If I respond, that's a slam on me. There's an arrogance in that attitude."

Outline Your Information. Instead of talking off the top of your head, or reading from a script, list the items that you want to say and group similar items together. Then write the main points on an index card and touch on them in your natural speaking voice. That way, you'll sound natural in your delivery without interjecting the fact that you love vintage cars between your hair color and marital status. This will also help the listener follow you, so he or she can refer to the information in any follow-up conversations. Also be sure to include the phone number where you can be reached as the last item on your list. Many times, out of nervousness, respondents hang up before leaving this vital piece of information!

Don't Overthink Your Message. It's easy to get caught up in wondering and trying to make everything perfect. You know the thought pattern: "If I say this or that, what will they think about me?" But if you get caught up in overthinking your message and redoing it again and again, you probably won't give a clear impression. Instead, be yourself. Your message should reflect your style and your interests.

Be Creative. If a mailbox is filled with dozens of messages and you want to hear from the advertiser, then you need to stand out. Consider clever ways you could respond to an ad. Did the ad mention a favorite musician? What about playing that music in the background of your voice message? For instance, Bob, our opera singer from Chapter 3, sang a brief piece in his voice greeting. Refer back to Chapter 6 for more ideas because crafting your response is like writing an ad for a radio spot. The first few words should draw the listener into the rest of your message. But be careful. Too much effort could make you seem a little desperate.

Invite Contact. When a company advertises a product, it usually ends the ad with an invitation for you to call for information, redeem the coupon, or be the 100th customer on a given day. You can increase the likelihood that you'll have your message returned if you do the same thing. Your call to action can be this simple: "There's a lot more I'd like to talk with you about, so why don't you call me some night this week at 555-5555?" Or you can entice the advertiser with a free ticket to an upcoming concert—just don't make the freebie event the first date. (We'll talk more about that in Chapter 10.) Also tell the advertiser when you're most reachable and in what area you live.

Leave a Secure Phone Number. Ideally, an unlisted phone number is better, because it's safer. And some avid personal-ad users have installed an unlisted second line at home to receive calls. But if you can't do this and your home phone number is listed, then leave your work number if you can accept phone calls there. Just be aware that you won't want to discuss any unusual experiences where your coworkers can eavesdrop over a cubicle wall. Use a call to your office as a way to screen the advertiser and get his or her number. Then arrange to call the person back after work. Whatever you do, don't leave a friend's number; otherwise, the caller may think that you're married or living with someone.

Speak Clearly. Was his name Jim or Tim? What was that phone number? Is he tired of the *married* life or a *harried* life? The person getting your message may never know and that could affect his or her decision on whether to call you back. So make sure you speak clearly when you leave a message. Monica placed the following personal ad, received 31 replies, and nearly decided to forgo the opportunity to meet with one of the respondents because his message was difficult to understand.

> Pray naked. Love life. Far from fundamentalist and frigid, intriguing Christian virgin seeks soul mate for rich relationship. Woman of integrity, passion, and intensity, artist by nature, twenty something, Jane-of-all-trades (currently a bicycle mechanic), seeks her best friend, who is a man of gentleness, honesty, and hope, respects himself and others, and isn't frightened by faith or faithfulness.

How did this sabotage nearly happen? Well, one call came from a man with a Scottish accent. She found his message appealing. Monica called him back and left her phone number on his answering machine. He returned her call, but between the background noise and his Scottish accent, he was difficult to understand. In fact, Monica thought she heard him suggest she allow him to "get her laid."

Considering her virgin status, she had expected at least one message of this sort. She dismissed it but grew angrier and angrier until she decided to call him back and give him a piece of her mind. Since he wasn't home, she left a message and said, "If I did want to get laid, I wouldn't ask you because I know you have no penis 'cause you're all asshole."

To her surprise she later received a call from the Scotsman. He was puzzled. Could she have misunderstood him? He hadn't suggested anything of the kind and he apologized for the misunderstanding. He'd simply asked if she'd allow him to "call her late." They made up and planned a dinner date. The lesson: speak clearly.

Include a Disclaimer, if Necessary. Be sensitive to how you're being perceived. And realize that your message might need a disclaimer if there are circumstances that might lead the advertiser to hesitate on whether to call you back. For example, some voice-mail systems allow the advertiser to learn the time when a message was left. So if you're responding to an ad, you should know that some people we spoke with imagined that the messages left in the middle of the night were from perverts, the unemployed, insomniacs, and other misfits. Another circumstance that might require a disclaimer is when you're recovering from a cold and your voice sounds like Marlon Brando's or Elmer Fudd's. So how do you leave a disclaimer? Just explain your reason somewhere in the call. Simply tell the advertiser that you work late or that you're getting over a cold.

If You're Self-Conscious, Have Someone Else Speak for You. If you want someone else to record your response because you're self-conscious about your voice, it's OK. But have your substitute state that he or she is calling in your place (and note that more serious-minded advertisers might feel that you're being dishonest). Perhaps you can even make a joke out of it. You could have your friend present your message as if he or she was fixing you up because the ad was perfect for you and your friend knows you'd never call. The important thing is not to misrepresent who you are. Your prospect shouldn't expect you to sound like the voice on the message unless that's your voice.

Review Your Message. You have just recorded your message and you're sweating like you've just jogged for 60 minutes on a treadmill. You lost your place on your list of items and you're afraid that you repeated your age at least three times. You may have even said a four-letter word. And, you can't remember leaving a phone number. That's OK. The beauty of our computer-prompted telecommunications world is that you can make mistakes and then fix them without anyone finding out. At the end of recording a message, most voice-mail response systems will prompt you to review your message by pressing a certain number or symbol. You'll be presented with another list of options and if you'd like to rerecord it, you can do that as many times as you'd like.

Just remember, the meter is running. And you have to start all over at the beginning of your message. Then when you feel comfortable with your message, it's also important to *send it*. That's because most voice-mail systems don't forward messages until the sender actually chooses that option.

Written Responses

While the written-response method is less popular, it is also less expensive, and it can be a much more intimate and friendly way of introducing yourself. What's more, the letters can also serve as a log of your courtship. That's what happened to Peter and Claira. As you may recall, we first met them in Chapter 2. When Claira decided to reply to Peter's ad, she had just gotten out of a bad romance and wasn't having much luck meeting anyone new. So she decided to try the personals. Peter's ad had asked for a written response and, since she felt comfortable in that arena, she thought she would respond. "I certainly could write a letter," she said. In addition to the request for a written response, she liked the fact that Peter was looking for "quality, not quantity" time. "That caught my eye," she said. "My life was busy. I was working six days a week, so it was good that he was up front about the amount of time." Here's her first letter, which was handwritten:

Hello! My name is Claira. I saw your ad and it really caught my attention—especially the part about having an "interesting, demanding life." Well, that's me.

Just to tell you a little more about myself, I am currently teaching a reading/writing course. I am diligently trying to finish up my masters degree; this is my last year. I am an intern at a local hospital on the weekends. I am also a teacher's assistant at school. The saving grace of doing all these things is that I really love what I am doing and I figure that the experience and ambition will eventually pay off.

I'm also fit and active—I love to play volleyball, and I'm in a league on Monday nights. Oh—I'm about 5'7", green eyes, auburn hair, 23 years old. I'm ambitious, open-minded, self-confident, optimistic. I've been here for about a year now (since last August), and I'm originally from out East. (My family is still there.) I live in a suburb now with my roommate who moved out here with me (we went to the same undergrad together). We have one cat.

I like it here but haven't gotten to see a whole lot yet. Some plays, a couple of museums, etc. (Do you like plays/theater?) Well, I've never done this thing before, but I thought I'd give it a shot, since your ad really resonated with me. Perhaps writing is a little less intimidating than trying to leave a message!

If you wouldn't mind, I would really like you to write back to me, before we get to meet. Besides the fact that I like the anticipation of waiting to get mail, I'd really like to get a better sense of the kinds of things you like to do, where you work, etc.

Plus, the way I look at it is, all we have is time! Friendships and relationships are like a slow dance, with each person getting to know the other a little at a time. A letter tends to allow a person more space to introduce themselves, without interruption.

And so . . . the dance begins.

I look forward to hearing from you, and hope you are keeping your stress level down to a minimum.

Claira said that this letter came easily and naturally. "I believe all things happen for a reason," she said. "So I was just sincere, open, and honest. And I just told everything that was going on in my life." This letter interested Peter, so he wrote back:

Nice letter! Nice idea, too—that I should return the favor, sending you a letter back. Turnabout being fair play, here I go.

Guess what? I live about seven blocks north of you. Heck, I may even deliver this letter by hand while out for a run!

I run a lot, incidentally, both for exercise and to ease the tensions of an "interesting, demanding life"—something you clearly know a thing or two about yourself.

Bad news: I'm allergic to cats. But I try not to hold it against 'em.

I'm 6'2" w/black hair and blue eyes. I work in journalism and P.R. downtown. In my spare time, I write (screenplays & fiction), occasionally act (in independent, locally produced videos and films), and run. I also enjoy movies (got my MA in film), dining, dancing (nothing fancy, just rock), and spending time with people who are unafraid to be themselves.

Also, I donate my time (what's left of it) to a low-income household I've been helping out for some time. Challenging, fulfilling, emotionally draining, but necessary.

Oh, and I have lousy penmanship. Perhaps you've figured that out already.

At any rate, your letter had a lot of personality; I was impressed. I'm also a pushover for green eyes. (Draw your own conclusions.)

—Peter [who then included his phone number].

When Claira received his letter, she was excited. "I thought it was pretty cool," she said. "I read it to my roommate who said that it was too good to be true." Claira also noticed that Peter had hand-delivered the letter. Since one of the reasons she wanted Peter to write a letter was so they could be on equal footing, she decided that she too needed to hand-deliver a letter. "I thought, he knows where I live, it's only fair to know where he lives," she said. She also found it pretty amazing that she lived so close to him. Here's her response to Peter's letter:

Hello! I got your letter this morning, and was psyched to find out that you live a mere seven blocks away. That should make getting together a good deal easier!

OK, getting down to business. I suppose I have taken the easy way out by dropping you a note as opposed to calling or leaving a message. However, this feels conspicuously like a blind date, which adds to the anticipation of a first meeting. (Besides, the fact that you live so close made it easy to drop this off.)

Time and place are flexible; however, my roommate and I are moving down one floor this weekend, to a larger apartment (which makes things a little more difficult than usual).

I don't know what your schedule looks like, but—what do you think about meeting on Saturday night or Wednesday night for dinner or coffee? (Sunday, I work and have to baby-sit; Monday, I play volleyball, but not till 9:15 P.M.)

Anyway, let me know what's good, even next week sometime.

(Feel free to call or leave a message, unless you prefer to leave notes the "pony express way", like we've been doing.) [She included her phone number.]

Talk to you soon.

Ironically, Peter didn't talk with her. Instead, he wrote the following note one day later.

Gee, it's been so long since we've spoken, I've forgotten the sound of your voice. Oh, that's right—I've never heard it!

I pretty much assumed that, after I wrote to you as "instructed," you'd be replying by phone. As shocked as you probably were to find yesterday's hand-delivery, I was equally stunned to receive yours back! After reading it, my first inclination was to pick up the receiver and be done with this protracted mutual-tease/mystery thing. But then the WEIRDNESS of it suddenly seemed too valuable a thing to squander.

So it's Saturday afternoon, and I'm taking a break from revising a short story. Later in this same break (long break, isn't it?), I'll put on the requisite running garb and deny the U.S. Postal Service yet another 29¢. (Between us, you and I are in danger of undoing Mr. Clinton's concerted efforts at reining in the budget deficit!)

I'm busy tonight but would love to take you to dinner (my treat—I'm the one who started all this!) either Monday (pre-V-ball) or Wednesday. Preferably the former.

OK, green eyes, the ball's set to you: spike it back where you will!

So where did she spike it? Back to him of course. Since she enjoyed writing and receiving the letters so much, she decided to write another letter and used it to set up the date (written and delivered on the same day that she received her letter):

Hi! Perhaps you expected this; we've probably gotten ourselves into a pattern now! But you're right, the uniqueness of our situation has been pretty interesting—so I'm continuing to take advantage of it!

I had a long day today—working as a teaching assistant; then coming home to find my apartment in disarray because of our move. Geez! Moving is always a hassle, but it's nice to go through the stuff I've been putting off forever.

Well . . . Monday, "pre-volleyball" sounds fine. Actually, if you wouldn't mind, you could even drop me off there after dinner, if that would give us more time. (I'll bring my knee pads with me, as opposed to wearing them to dinner.)

Here's the plan: you could meet me at my place at about/between 6:45–7:00 P.M. Monday, and we could go from there. (I would tell you how to get here, but you seem to have figured that out pretty well!)

Feel free to break the pattern and confirm by phone, if the feeling so moves you (isn't it getting a little chilly for running shorts?).

Continuing in their virtual volleyball game of letters, Peter responded with the following letter the next day to confirm their date:

If I've ever written three letters to the same person within such a short time span, I'm not aware of it. But I did want us to meet on equal footing, so as of this moment we are tied at 3 correspondences apiece. Now STOP! (If you want to.)

Certainly I can drop you off after dinner. By the way, I used to play in a league myself; a few years ago I was a better-than-average V-baller cursed, tragically, with weaker-than-average ankles. I kept jumping high at the net & landing wrong (primarily on other people's feet). After my third sprain I decided to stick w/running. Sad tale, huh? I'm enclosing a Kleenex just in case.

Hope your move went/is going smoothly & without incident. I hate moving! Before coming to this place, I lived in the same apartment for nine years!

Your letters have been charming and enjoyable, and I'm very much looking forward to meeting their author. I'll be there at 6:45 sharp!

Their date, needless to say, went well. "We were certainly more comfortable than if we had been on a blind date," Claira said and credited that to all the letters that they had exchanged. "It was a nice way to get to know each other." She was also pleasantly surprised that they had even more in common than the letters promised. "It was important for me to find someone with strong spirituality," she said. "Peter hadn't mentioned that in his ad—to have a spiritual basis in the relationship—but he did mention it on the date. So I got lucky that we have a similar outlook on the importance of God in our lives." Since the date went so well, she decided to thank Peter for it in one more letter the day after they met.

How are you doing?

I am by no means trying to be one up on you as far as letters go, but since I really enjoyed our written as well as verbal communication, I thought I'd keep going a little further, before the winter weather sets in! (Besides, I enjoy writing/receiving mail type stuff.)

Straight to the point—thanks for dinner. I really enjoyed your company (and you do look younger than your age). I'm looking forward to talking with you and getting together on Friday.

How was your day? Mine was terribly stressful. My students just don't seem to be getting what I'm teaching, and it can be really draining. I'm sure we're making progress in their writing. I just want it to be quicker!

Anyway, all is well, and I'm looking forward to talking to you soon . . .

Since you'll probably get this Wed. (A.M.)—hope you have a good day!

Of her experience, Claira said, "It all came together. I saw the ad at the right time in my life. It was the first and only ad that I answered." Their relationship grew and evolved from there and two years and two days after their first date, they married.

Now that we have seen an example of a successful early courtship through letters, let's look at some of the success secrets for using the mail. Please note that these success secrets work for on-line responses as well.

Focus Your Response on the Type of Person You Want to Meet. It's that simple. It's better to focus your response on the type of person you really want to meet than on yourself or trying to make yourself sound like you fully fit into the requirements of a specific ad. Neil learned this lesson when he began responding to ads with this letter.

Hi. I'm Neil, a successful company president, 5'8", 145#, 30s, with a full mustache and beard; trim, muscular physique; and excellent health. I'm a warm, caring, understanding, sensuous, sexy, romantic, adventurous, intelligent, witty, and fun-loving, red-blooded American boy.

I'm looking for similar qualities in a young (18–36), attractive, sexy, slender, affectionate, honest, and sincere woman with no dependents (living with you). If things work out between us, I would invite you to live with me on my beautiful estate. I'm looking for a long-term monogamous relationship; since I don't drink, smoke, or do drugs, it would be really great to find a woman that also cares about her health.

Since you would be relocating here it only makes sense to tell you a little bit about your new lifestyle and home. It is set out much like a country club or golf course, with over 400 trees including many magnificent evergreens and white birch. Some of the amenities on the property include a large building housing a year-round swimming pool with diving board and slide, a large whirlpool Jacuzzi spa, and a sauna. Adjacent to the pool building is a basketball court that doubles as a heliport, tennis court, ice skating rink, and go-cart racetrack. The outside toys include a 3-wheel all-terrain vehicle, dirt bike, and golf cart. In the main house we'll view a 6 1/2-foot big-screen TV hooked up to a super stereo system and a video recorder with color camera from the comfort of a kidney-shaped waterbed couch. Perhaps we'll play a game of pool, Ping Pong, or air hockey before we work out with the exercise equipment. We'll relax in front of one of the six fireplaces and perhaps barbecue some filet mignon in the hibachi in the fireplace. A perfect setting for the beautiful romantic evening. Shall we dip in the hot, bubbly spa later?

In the morning we may take off in the Titan, a deluxe 27-foot motor home with all the latest electronic gadgets including phone, heat, electricity, kitchen, etc. We'll go on many enjoyable camping trips in this neat vehicle.

Occasionally, we may just fly off to some romantic tropical island for the weekend.

When my two little girls come to visit every other weekend, we'll all do "family things." Do you like kids?

I guess what I'm saying is that I'm offering a complete package. A great guy. A nice family life. A beautiful comfortable lifestyle. Possibly even a job if you'd like. Now it's your turn to tell me why you should be my woman.

If you meet my qualifications and I meet yours and you want to start a new life and bring some happiness into your life, please call. Let me know your age, height, weight, measurements, and what type of relationship you desire.

On the other side of the page was an aerial view of his estate with all points of interest clearly labeled. He also included a color photo of himself. And with all the emphasis on his stuff, guess who Neil attracted. That's right, gold diggers. If he'd focused more on the values and interests of the person he wanted to meet, perhaps he would have been more successful.

Acknowledge Part of the Ad. Many advertisers feel that some of the responses they get, especially written ones, are mass mailings. And indeed some respondents do write stock responses and record or mail them to many advertisers. But this can backfire. When Liz and her friend placed an ad in the same publication, they both received the same form letter from one respondent—not exactly a romantic approach nor a very appealing one. And while using a stock letter is an easy way to respond to a lot of ads, it's not necessarily a very effective way to connect. In fact, many of the advertisers we interviewed said they're most likely to respond to people who reference a point they've made in their ad or message. Then they know that the interest is genuine. You can even cover more ground and have a higher response rate if you combine the two approaches. Create your response, and leave time to weave in information addressing a few of the items from the ad or voice message. That way you can talk about yourself—and let the advertiser know what you're looking for in a relationship—while you let the advertiser know why his or her ad caught your attention. For an example, look again at Claira's first letter. She clearly read Peter's ad—and then responded to specific points in it.

Be Creative. If you're connecting on-line, and have access to a scanner, you can send an image of yourself, a bouquet of flowers, or even a favorite cartoon. Or you can add a bit of creativity with symbols known as emoticons. Here's a rose: -<—<—@ (For more emoticons, see Appendix B.) Additionally, your letter or on-line response is like a direct-response sales letter. The first few words should draw your reader into the body copy. It's just like crafting an ad, so if you skipped Chapter 6, go back and read it for suggestions on writing copy.

Leave Him or Her Wanting More. After all, why would anyone want to meet you if he or she didn't want to know more? So don't overwhelm people with your response. But remember, if you're writing a letter or e-mail message, many people prefer that a respondent takes the time to write a page or two. They feel that a lengthy response indicates a more thoughtful person. By sharing more information about yourself, you may present some information that will strike a chord with the advertiser. For instance, one person we interviewed received a response from a woman who mentioned his favorite book. They struck up an e-mail conversation discussing aspects of the story. Now, they plan to meet because of their exchange. But throughout their exchange, they didn't say everything in any one letter. This gave the other person a chance to respond and continue the exchange.

Consider the Paper You Use. Loose-leaf paper or a greeting card? This is a question many respondents ask themselves. A page torn from a spiral binder will leave a much different impression than an artful—or humorous—greeting card. Erica, a 27-year-old graphic designer, knew this well from her professional life. While she'd never considered answering an ad, she read the personals for amusement. But then one day she found an ad that piqued her interest. So she called the advertiser and waited. No response.

Five months later, Erica was throwing away some newspapers and saw the same ad in that week's edition. She felt fate telling her to call again. So she called and left a message. Eight days later she received a message from Ed, the guy who had placed the ad. Over several weeks, they played phone tag and had several conversations. In order to meet, Ed requested that Erica send him an extraordinary letter that would entice him enough to want to meet. Being a creative person, Erica enjoyed the challenge and put together a package that included two photos, a cassette tape of some of her favorite tunes, and this humorous multiple choice quiz about herself.

A page from Erica's response package

Oz is:
- ○ a singer that Erica has on tape
- ○ Erica's cat
- ○ Erica's cranky next-door neighbor

Erica once went to see:
- ○ Tom Jones
- ○ M. C. Hammer
- ○ Cher
- ○ none of the above
- ○ all of the above

Of the following, Erica likes to read which best:
- ○ *People*
- ○ *New Age* magazine
- ○ *Playgirl*

When Erica dances, she shakes:
- ○ her butt
- ○ her arms
- ○ her boobs
- ○ all of the above

Erica likes guys who:
- ○ are funny
- ○ can dance
- ○ give good massages
- ○ have nice chests
- ○ all of the above
- ○ none of the above

One of Erica's worst habits is:
- ○ singing in the car while driving
- ○ procrastination
- ○ fear and self-doubt

Erica thinks too many people today are:
- ○ unhappy with their jobs
- ○ not spiritual enough
- ○ needlessly afraid to dance
- ○ all of the above

Erica reads a lot of:
- ○ fiction
- ○ metaphysical and mind stuff
- ○ love stories

Erica loves:
- ○ reading
- ○ dancing
- ○ sweets

Erica's niece's name is
- ○ Stephanie
- ○ Megan
- ○ Andrea

Erica's into:
- ○ feng shui
- ○ numerology
- ○ the angels
- ○ all of the above

Erica's favorite male actor is:
O Clint Eastwood
O Tom Cruise
O Jimmy Smits
O none; she doesn't have a favorite

Erica is irritated by:
O tardiness
O typos
O slowpoke drivers
O all of the above

Erica wears perfume:
O always
O sometimes
O rarely
O never

Which of the following does Erica like best:
O baseball
O basketball
O football

Erica has a lot of which color in her wardrobe:
O off white
O red
O blue

Erica generally wears what to bed:
O T-shirts and undies
O men's boxers
O Victoria's Secret stuff
O all of the above

Someone recently told Erica she has a large:
O bra collection
O crystal collection
O lipstick collection

In high school, Erica was:
O quiet
O wild
O shy

Erica absolutely hates:
O doing dishes
O cutting the grass
O doing laundry

Erica thinks she is:
O psychic
O a weirdo
O going to be famous someday
O all of the above

She sent this response package to Ed. And nine days later, he got back to her and said that he enjoyed her package. They then made plans to meet.

Aim for a Warm Personal Impression. If your handwriting is neat and legible, use it, because a handwritten note leaves a warmer, more personal impression. But if you are more inclined to write like a cave dweller, a typed note will spare the reader from trying to decipher your message. You can still warm up your message by including a photograph or favorite cartoon and by using a good-quality paper. Whichever method you choose, first write out your message on scrap paper, so you don't make a mess out of your final draft.

Flick Your Pic

Today, photographs can play a part in any media you choose. Newspaper advertisers exchange them by mail. Internet users can send digital images back and forth in minutes via their computers. When it comes to taking your picture, consider the following suggestions.

- Wear the clothing that fits your personality and your everyday lifestyle—or at least a lifestyle that you aspire to. Don't send a picture of yourself in formal wear if you feel as though you are being tortured any time you are required to wear such an outfit. Remember that people want to see what you're really like.
- Be playful. Use a picture of yourself as a child. Show a pet. But remember that if you don't show yourself, some people will think that you're either extraordinarily ugly or extraordinarily arrogant.
- Be sensitive to the environment you're in. You may have a picture of yourself that looks complimentary, but the room it was taken in was a mess. If you don't have an opportunity to clarify that you're not the slob, use a different picture. On the other hand, if that's the real you, go for it. It may cost you a few responses; however, the responses you do get should be more accepting of your organizational habits.
- Avoid overtly sexual photos. For the most part, pictures of body parts, nudity, or bikini shots scare more people than they entice.

- Use a picture that's a reasonable facsimile of you. One of the biggest complaints that we hear about the personals is that pictures that people receive are often outdated and were obviously taken when the subjects were younger, weighed less, and had fewer wrinkles and more hair. Don't lead a respondent to a disappointing meeting because that won't do you any good, either.
- Note your camera angles. A camera pointed down at you from above will make you look more approachable and accepting— while a camera pointed up at you will give you a more authoritative demeanor.

Eliminate Your Return Address. If you're responding to an ad by mail, do not place your return address on the envelope. Inside the letter, you can mention the area where you reside or work. That way you're less vulnerable. And if by chance the letter is lost in the mail, just figure it wasn't meant to be. (For more security precautions, see Chapter 9.)

Live Your Life

Once you've responded to an ad or even a group of ads, don't wait for the e-mail or phone calls to start pouring in—and don't close yourself off from meeting people by other means. Personal ads are just one way of meeting people, but the experience may help in other ways, giving you more confidence to meet someone at a bar or a party. In fact, when you respond to an ad, there are two things you must always remember:

1. **Get on with your other activities.** If you've left several voice-mail messages or written a letter or two, you may feel inclined to head straight home after work—instead of to the health club or volunteer activity—so you can check your messages and mail. But you shouldn't do this—you shouldn't stop your life for anyone, least of all strangers. Go about your business and accept that whatever happens is what's meant to happen. If someone wants to get a hold of you, he or she will. The few that go by while you're doing your other activities won't matter in the long run.

2. **Handle rejection with finesse.** Now it's been five days since you left your message and there's been no response. You may be tempted to call the mailbox again. In most cases, that would be a waste of energy. Don't dwell on what you could have done or said differently. Chances are good that the reason you didn't get a response was because you live too far away or there was another factor that had little to do with your value as a date. The personals, like any other way to meet a potential date, are really a numbers game, so simply call more numbers. If, after responding to about 20 ads you've never gotten a response, it may help you to share the situation with a friend for feedback. As we've already mentioned, it's easier to avoid feeling anxious about whether you'll receive a particular response when you've left a bunch of messages.

8

The Fair
and the Square:
Finding the Winners

Kaye, a 37-year-old controller for an accounting firm, had pretty much given up on meeting Mr. Right. Most of her friends had married. The men in bars were 10 years younger than she was. But with a close friend's prodding, she placed an ad.

> Blue-eyed blonde, slim and fit professional loves anything outdoors in warm weather and near water. Hobbies include sailing, golf, running, cycling, travel, film, theater and the Cubbies. Looking for 35–42 S/DWM that is attractive, bright, active, social, financially secure, unpretentious, honest, chivalrous and a sense of humor wouldn't hurt! Marriage, etc., etc., well, I thought we'd see if we like each other first.

She received about 17 voice-mail responses within two weeks. One introduced himself as "Racey" and said, "You should know that the speed of the pack is determined by the lead dog." He then made a point of telling Kaye that he bet his message would be her first. He told very little about himself and ended with, "You know the mind is like a parachute—it's not functional until it's opened up!"

Kaye interpreted his energy and enthusiasm as a sign of desperation. "If I had liked the sound of his voice," she said, "I would have called him no matter how many calls I had received."

Another caller worked in a steel mill and didn't leave much of an impression. Other calls came from men who were not of the ethnic or religious background she was seeking.

Then Kaye got a message from Dale. She was intrigued by this 38-year-old investment firm partner. He was divorced and had just moved to the city. When she called him, he said all the right things, so they met for dinner. They had an easy conversation. He was sensitive, articulate, and didn't push her for her phone number. They talked a little about where they worked and their interests—of which they had many in common—and Kaye liked the fact that he didn't bash his ex-wife.

But Kaye was determined to keep all her options open, so she also returned a call from Pete—a 39-year-old divorced stockbroker who'd said that he left his work at the office. She liked that attitude. But when she called, he immediately asked if she was the one who was into scuba diving. To her credit, she wasn't annoyed that her ad was not the only one that had sparked his interest. She met Pete for lunch, but she found it suspicious that he didn't eat.

Meanwhile, Dale tracked Kaye down at work and asked her for another date. She was impressed that he'd reached her because she hadn't even given him her last name. She met him a second time, but now he seemed a bit cooler—or at least he didn't make a move to advance the relationship.

An accountant was about the *last* person Kaye wanted to date, but because Trent, an IRS agent, was one of the first messages she received, she returned his call. He was 42 and had never married. They enjoyed conversation over a drink. He was nice, but she wasn't moved.

Another call came from James, a 38-year-old computer consultant. They shared a few common interests. So after a brief phone conversation, they met for dinner. She found him entertaining enough, but he monopolized the conversation. He also picked up the check and proceeded to ask her to a movie. Since he suggested a day right then, she felt obligated to accept, but the date immediately seemed to be looming on her calendar.

Kaye was starting to get confused. Which one had worked for the IRS? Who was the one who had recently divorced? Luckily, true to her accountant skills, she had recorded all the calls and dates on a legal pad. And she wasn't ready to give up. She proceeded to return another call, this one from Hank. An athletic, good-natured, intelligent, traditional guy—that's how Hank described himself. His voice had a nice quality and he also expressed an interest in some of the things she'd mentioned.

During their first conversation—which lasted for about 15 minutes—Kaye found him to be exceptionally quiet. He seemed nervous, but she was curious and agreed to meet him again, this time for dinner. After a few beers and a lively political discussion he loosened up and she found that he had a good mind and a great sense of humor.

Through these experiences, just like George in Chapter 6, Kaye was able to discover what she really wanted in a relationship. "You know, the men I'd called back fit the description of who I was looking for," she said. "Yet, they were nothing like the two men who were really important to me in the past." A friend told her that she was sensing Kaye had a fresh new attitude. And Kaye admitted that even if she didn't find the relationship that she wanted with this ad, she was open to trying it again.

Odds are, if you place a personal ad, you'll get responses—and you might even get more responses than you can handle—which can be exciting. Heck, even one response can be exciting. (If you are one of the small percentage of people who receive no responses, go back through Chapters 5 and 6; you probably just need to make different media choices or tweak your copy.) But like Kaye, you might start getting confused by trying to keep all the messages straight. Which message did you like? On which date did you meet so-and-so? Where did you go with so-and-so? It's hard to keep this organized. And harder still if you get a lot of responses. How do you choose which to call back so you can make the most of these new opportunities? The answers are easier than you may think.

When we asked advertisers to estimate the percentage of responses that were promising, so-so, and "not-if-he/she-was-the-last-person-on-earth," we found that a third of the responses fell into each category. And for most people, the reject pile was fairly obvious. It consisted of letters from people who had sent nude photos of themselves or close-ups of body parts; phone messages that came across as being too seductive for a first encounter; or simply people whose location, age, or lifestyle qualities were beyond the advertiser's acceptable standards.

The responses that fall into either the middle or promising categories are harder to identify immediately, although there are some clues. Put the responses of people who, while they may seem nice, don't create any sparks into the middle, or so-so, category. Often the responses that are more clever or, more importantly, are more directly linked to the advertiser's specifications go in the top—or most promising—category.

Although we lack any scientific data, we've heard that you can expect 33 percent of your responses to be promising. If you find that less than a third of your responses fall into this category, what does that mean? Well, assuming your media choice was right on target, then perhaps your ad needs refining.

If, however, you receive a high number of responses that fall into the promising category—resulting in having more callbacks than you can manage— perhaps you were not screening as thoroughly as you should have been.

And, finally, if most of the responses you get fall into the so-so pile, take a hard look at your ad. Or let a friend read it. Ask for an honest opinion. You may be surprised. Then play with your ad. Try different words. A more creative twist. A different publication. Do this before you swear off dating through the personals. And above all, even if you get a small percentage of promising responses, give them a chance. As we have already said, you only need to find one promising respondent to make your entire experience worthwhile.

But assuming you do get promising responses, what do you do next? How do you get the most out of the experience? And how do you keep track of all of the responses—even the rejected ones? It's easy if you simply get organized.

Document Your Responses

You may think you'll remember the people who respond to your ad, but most advertisers are surprised at how easily they lose control of the process. Think about it. Do you recall interviewing for several jobs within a short time period? After only three or four interviews, you probably couldn't remember which responsibilities, salary, or benefits pertained to which position. That's one reason why organized interviewees take notes. It's the same with the personals. So here are some tips that will help prevent confusion and maybe even some embarrassment.

Create a Log

Before you even pick up your first phone message, you need to be organized. That means setting up a system to track all your responses and dating experiences. Start by creating a file where you can record:

- Your ads, so that you can later determine which one was the most successful
- The publications and other places where you ran your ad, so you can identify the best media vehicle for you
- The dates you ran your ad and the date each response was received
- The respondent's name, address, phone, employer, work phone, age, marital status, and children, if any
- Relevant health issues that can range from allergies to physical disabilities to HIV status
- Key facts—including occupation and hobbies—that will help you remember each respondent
- The date you contacted the individual, any meeting arrangements, and the outcome

You'll find yourself scribbling comments like "No way!" or "Meet this one!" in the corners of your log, so it would be good to set up a quick-reference section so that you can check all of your impressions at a glance. If you log each response on a separate page, keep all of the pages together in a file folder or three-ring binder. (See Appendix D for a sample form.) If you're accepting written responses as well, save the letters, faxes, or cards, but also fill out the form for each respondent. Then you'll have all of the information in one place and no one will fall through the cracks.

Once you set up your log, you have to be sure to record *all* of the responses—even the people you do not want to meet: a woman who sounds like the actress Fran Drescher; a man who decides to tell you about his matchbook collection—in detail; and anyone who makes unwelcome explicit sexual invitations.

When you pick up your responses, you'll probably receive some that you just want to skip. But whether you plan to return a call or not, you should keep track of it. And if you don't plan to follow up with some, you should note the reason why. This is a good idea for several reasons.

- People tend to reply to similar ads. If you run another ad months later—even in a different publication—you may attract a response from someone you already eliminated from your list of possibilities. And if you have some information about the previous responses and why you eliminated that person, it will save you some time, as well as some possible heartache.
- If you run several ads, you can compare the quality and quantity of the responses that each ad attracted. (The same goes for testing the results in different mediums.)
- Subsequent responses might seem more appealing. Maybe you didn't want to follow up because he or she was recently divorced. If you hear from the individual again, he or she might not mention it, but you'll know. If you hear from this person a year or more later, maybe you'll feel more comfortable about meeting.
- Some respondents leave multiple messages in voice-mail boxes when they don't get a return call. The respondent may even use threats and insults to glean a response from you. In the unlikely event that you encounter one of these desperately driven singles, you should report him or her to the service handling the calls. Your record of the calls will help document the incident.
- You might change your mind about an individual and then want to get back to him or her.

Listen Carefully to Voice-Mail Responses

Most voice-mail systems are going to charge you by the minute to retrieve your messages, so pay attention. You don't want to have to repeat your fourth message because you were having fantasies about message three. This is your first opportunity to learn everything possible about the callers—your potential mates. And their responses can provide you with something to talk about should you decide to return their calls.

You may want to listen to the callers first, then go back and record the information. Have your forms ready and take notes. Write down the phone numbers correctly. And make sure you match the correct names with the correct phone numbers. Then, with each response, you should note the following.

The Voice. This may tell you a lot about the individual. Most basically, it can tell you if the caller can communicate with you. Liz, a 36-year-old public relations professional in Georgia, received a call from a man who mumbled his entire message. She couldn't understand anything he had to say. Naturally, she couldn't—and she wouldn't—return this call. Would you? Analyze the voice. Is it natural as well as relaxed? Nervous? Smooth? Energetic? Laid-back? Is there an accent? Does the person sound older or younger than the age? Does the caller sound open or cautious? Does he or she hesitate or stumble over words? Is he or she giggling between phrases? Does he or she convey a positive or a negative attitude? Remember, as we mentioned earlier, don't assume that a sexy, energetic, smooth voice is coming from a sexy, energetic, smooth individual. At this point, you don't have enough information to judge why one caller sounds different from another, just note it.

The Facts. Of course, the content of the call is also relevant. Do the qualities that the individual describes match the qualities in your ad? Does he or she specifically say why your ad was chosen? Where does he or she live? Are the facts consistent? For example, did the person state that he or she just moved to the area but also that he or she has been in the same job for three years? If everything else seems OK, don't automatically assume the person is lying (he or she could, for example, have been transferred to the area). So, instead, if you decide to call him or her back, ask about it. Evaluate the response in terms of the tone the person uses as much as the explicit explanation. Be wary of a defensive attitude that may stop you from asking more questions. Another very important question if the respondent left a beeper number: Why? Is he or she trying to hide something, including a spouse? Or was that number given out for accessibility or to protect himself or herself as much as you're trying to protect yourself?

The Background Noise. Is he or she calling from a cell phone? Is the person near traffic or heavy equipment? Are there children in the background? Is a dog barking? Can you hear music? What type? A television? Be observant. If the voice-mail message includes a time stamp, what time did the caller leave the message? These are all important clues that can help feed your intuition about the individual. So pay attention.

Read Between the Lines with Written Responses

When newspaper personal ads rely on letters as the response vehicle, the paper or stationery and handwriting offer clues to a person's identity. As we explained in Chapter 7, someone who scribbles a note on loose-leaf paper is probably very different in personality from someone who sends a note in a sophisticated greeting card.

Of course, as with phone responses, the content is the most relevant aspect. Do the qualities that the individual describes match the qualities you're seeking? Does he or she specifically say why he or she chose your ad? Where does this person live? Are the facts consistent?

What about the tone of the letter? Is it friendly? Funny? Hurried? Disorganized? The more observations you can make about the individual, the better. And all of these points are clues to feed your intuition.

Written responses also offer a chance to exchange pictures. And this is becoming even more important for people with computers who respond via e-mail. In addition, many people who use computers have access to scanners, so they can create digital, transferable copies of their photos and post them on-line. In fact, on-line services have libraries filled with photos of single people. And while these can be as misleading as descriptions, they can help you learn a lot about the individual.

Naturally a picture can give you an idea of a person's appearance. But you can also note how this person wants you to perceive him or her. Was the picture taken at a formal event? Or was the person in the wilderness? Was he or she photographed with a child? With a pet? Was the photo taken in his or her home? If so, what sort of an environment is it? Does it fit with the information in the response? Are there other people in the shot? Is the pose seductive? Did he or she pose in front of a car or a house? What was he or she wearing?

Then try to determine reality. Many personal-ad users warn that the photos they receive are often inaccurate. Some were taken years earlier. Others were taken before the person put on 30 pounds. And few post a photo that represents how they look on an average day.

Don't Expect Fireworks

Relationship expert Susan Page suggests that people should meet with anyone who is even mildly interesting because sometimes it takes a while to fall in love. That turned out to be the right advice for Betty. A writer, who'd divorced after 23 years of marriage and three children, she found that she wanted friends who would be interested in backpacking along a favorite California river with her. She also hoped that, in a group of friends with similar interests, she just might find romance. So she placed a personal ad in a local paper and wrote, "Wind River man needed for romantic hiking partner."

Meanwhile, Bill, a 50ish philosophy professor and jazz musician, wrote an ad with the headline, "Youth is wasted on the young." He thought that he might attract the attention of the sort of woman he wanted with this headline. It did. While waiting for the results of her own ad, Betty responded to Bill's and they met in a coffee shop. Betty was intrigued, but not sold. But over time Betty found him to be sweet and trustworthy, and now they've been seeing each other for over two years.

Like Betty, you may decide to give a relationship some time but remember, there's also a fine line between giving romance time to develop and settling for someone who makes you feel less than wonderful. If you're not feeling satisfied with the people that you are meeting, go back to your list of needs. See if your descriptions need updating. Also feel free to change them if you discover something new about what's important to you. Let the list evolve. But don't overlook your needs in order to make a relationship work. If you do, it won't work for long. So don't settle for less than what you truly want and need to be happy.

When you finally decide which responses deserve a follow-up call, go for it! Ask questions. Conduct it as you would a phone interview. You want to get as much information as possible. You want to discover what your respondents are all about.

At this stage, you have all the control. And you can do one of two things with that: Maintain it or lose it. Maintaining control ensures your safety. There's nothing wrong with having a few phone conversations in order for you to feel absolutely comfortable with a person before revealing your phone number or address. You can build trust by observing whether the respondent can keep a phone date. And if the facts this person presents are consistent from one conversation to the next. If they are, this person will gain credibility. If they aren't, get out!

So who should you be looking for at this stage? It's up to you. John from Chapter 6 got back to everyone and left getting together for coffee up to the respondent. He felt that it was only fair. "They took a risk," he said. "So it was the right thing to do." George, on the other hand, used this time to screen out people, before deciding whether to meet for coffee. "I would ask three questions," he said. "What's your favorite restaurant? Where did you go on your last vacation? And what recent movies did you like?" Why these three questions? Because he wanted to see how they talked about something that was unrehearsed. "I used this as an index of their intelligence and their comfort level with themselves."

Whether you offer to meet everyone who responds or make the choice to screen, there are some pointers you should consider when getting back to an individual.

Be Comfortable

The best way to return a phone call is to have some privacy and enough time for a leisurely conversation so you don't feel rushed. Don't try to return a phone call from your cubicle at work with five other people walking past your desk. If you sound hurried, you may sound evasive and you may scare the other person away. If you have to call back from work, do it, if possible, during a break or at lunchtime. And don't hold it against the individual that he or she requested a daytime phone call, because this person is probably just trying to be self-protective by giving out a work phone number.

Be Inquisitive Without Creating an Inquisition

Just as you would interview a candidate for a job, at some point you'll need to screen your applicants to verify your impressions. For this purpose, personal ads offer an advantage over traditional dating. You can ask questions that are more personal sooner than you can in a traditional dating situation.

Since the only reason you're communicating with this person is to explore the possibility of starting a new relationship, you can clarify expectations and explore a person's background and interests right in the first step. So ask about previous relationships. Are there any patterns? What does that say about him or her? Who does he or she blame for the breakup of the previous relationships? Does the person complain about someone wanting commitment? Being too outgoing? Are his or her interests real or idealized? Maybe the person mentioned a passion for bowling, but the last time he or she bowled was 1984.

You can acquire more information when you offer the same information up front. If you want to find out why someone is divorced, tell him or her why you are unattached or divorced. Or talk about the divorce of an acquaintance. Often, giving just one simple but highly personal fact can open the door to a surprisingly honest dialogue.

Use the Response as a Conversation Starter

The task is to get beyond the awkward first moments of a conversation with someone new. So go ahead. Take your notes from your log and use them during the conversation. Refer to information that the person provided about himself or herself. You can even mention some of the background noises that you noticed. For instance, when you talk to the person, you can say, "You know, I noticed that you had a game on in the background. Was it the Bulls from last Sunday? What did you think of it?" That should get the person going.

Screen for Type of Relationship

Susan Page, author of *If I'm So Wonderful Why Am I Still Single?*, suggested screening for the relationship preference right at the beginning. No one should feel like he or she is being asked for a marriage proposal right off, but you can share an idea of what ultimately you want out of a dating relationship. Of course, even if you share this information, you'll still want a chance to get to know a partner before making any kind of commitment. But if you're definitely into *not* getting married or having children, the other person should know this from the start. Having this information saves everyone time—and, as we've mentioned, heartache.

Look for Red Flags

Does the information you've received during your phone conversation agree with the facts you got from the response? Or is there conflicting information? You may even note that a person contradicts himself or herself during a conversation or over the course of several conversations. Is he or she being too agreeable? This happens. Is the person being too pushy about meeting before he or she gets to know much about you? Has he or she left several messages or e-mails before you've had a chance to respond to one? After several conversations, does the person still insist that he or she can't share a home phone number? These are all signs that there may be some hidden agenda at work—an agenda that does not have your best interests at heart.

Don't Be Too Judgmental

If Todd, 39, received a message that was sent in the middle of the night, he was leery. He envisioned someone who was depressed or rejected or was an insomniac—one way or another, not his ideal person. But there are many reasons why someone might leave a late-night phone message. Some people, such as hospital employees, work odd hours. Others may have been motivated to leave a message after returning home from a date from hell. For some single parents, late at night could be the only time it's quiet enough to make such a call.

Then again it could mean something negative. Maybe you've received a call from a depressed, rejected insomniac. Or maybe that's the only time the caller can leave a message without his or her spouse listening in. Likewise, if you receive a call in the daytime, do you assume the person is unemployed?

These are all examples of the many ways we can interpret a situation. We can overanalyze. We judge on past experiences. We explain away inconsistencies. And we may even rationalize away warning signs. The lesson here is to be observant, but don't draw too many conclusions right way. Just use the information you get to find out more about a person's situation.

Trust Your Instincts

Your intuition will guide you far more than any policy you may have about dating. In our first book, *How to Succeed in Advertising When All You Have Is Talent,* Don Easdon, a successful advertising executive, told us, "I trust my instincts. You have to listen to your instincts and even though you feel inarticulate, just start talking about it. Trying to explain what you feel helps you get used to articulating what your gut is telling you." The same goes for dating. If your gut tells you something is wrong, then it probably is—even if you can rationalize the situation. So you need to recognize your intuition and trust it.

Answer to Yourself

Once you've decided to do something, don't worry about answering to friends or family. Playing the personals is currently not the dating convention. You're an explorer. Whether you're a conservative or liberal person, you'll become a quicker more accurate judge by practicing being in touch with those instincts. Then in the words of Nike, "Just do it."

Get Out When It's Not Clicking

The anonymity of personal ads can breed an instant intimacy that can undermine potential relationships. One personal-ad user described it this way, "You talk to someone for hours on-line. You graduate to a phone conversation. You eventually meet and poof! The fantasy is over."

Sometimes it doesn't even take that long. You may be talking with someone on the phone and realize his or her goals are very different from yours. In fact many of your calls will probably be from people you'll have no interest in pursuing. So you should learn how to exit gracefully from a conversation, so you're not wasting time. At that point, there is nothing wrong with stating your observation and wishing him or her well in the search.

The same is true for your caller. Some respondents may discover that you're not who they had in mind and that they have no interest in getting to know you better. Don't be hurt or offended by this. If each of you seem sincere but incompatible, you may want to keep the other person in mind for a friend.

Try, Try Again

There's no reason why you'd have to date any of your respondents. Don't just follow up with any responses if none of them feel right to you. If you don't receive the kind of responses you want, try again. You only invested a stamp, a few bucks for an ad, and some writing time. So you really didn't lose much. And every time you try it—if you keep refining your ad and your media selection—you're getting closer to your goal. That's part of the beauty of the personals.

9
Playing It Safe
While Playing the Personals

A coward is incapable of exhibiting love; it is the prerogative of the brave.

—Mahatma Gandhi

Back in September of 1992, *People* magazine reported the sad story of Roger Paulson. According to the article, a woman named Johnie Elaine Miller responded to a personal ad that this divorced 36-year-old sales rep had placed in a Washington, D.C., magazine. They hit it off and she moved in with him after just a few months of dating. Then while cleaning house, he discovered "dozens of false identity cards and drivers' licenses." Realizing that something wasn't right, he went to the FBI and learned that her true identity was Lisa Ann Rohn, a 28-year-old former prostitute who was wanted for credit card fraud. They arrested her and she spent six months in jail for possessing false identification.

Paulson continued to see her while she was in jail and he wrote her numerous love notes. But even though he had kept in touch with her, his infatuation with her started to wane. He began dating another woman. When Rohn was released from jail, however, he let her spend the night and the next day with him.

But the day after that, Paulson went off to see his new girlfriend and, in retaliation, Rohn picked up a guy in a bar and ended up spending the night with him. Deciding that he'd had enough, Paulson tossed all of Rohn's belongings out of his apartment and included a note telling her not to return. But when she did, she killed him.

This story, according to the article's author, should be seen as a warning to singles and further proof that the personals are a land of deception. But it wasn't the personals that brought Paulson to his fate. He could have just as easily met Rohn at a singles party, in a bar, or even through friends. At the risk of blaming the victim, he could have—and should have—stopped seeing Rohn when he learned that she was a fraud and was in jail (he clearly was conflicted about staying with her). Of course, as Gavin De Becker pointed out in his book *The Gift of Fear,* ending an abusive or potentially violent relationship is harder and more dangerous than starting one. At any rate, the fact that Paulson met Rohn through an ad is insignificant; the infinite number of ways that people get into healthy relationships are the same infinite number of ways that people get into violent ones.

Of course, this article isn't the only example of implying that dating through ads can be dangerous. Many popular movies, books, and novels play off this fear as well. Just look at the hit movie *Sea of Love.* Why is the idea of meeting someone dangerous through an ad so powerful? We believe that it's because the personals are so effective in breaking through the cocoon that we spend so many hours trying to construct in order to protect ourselves.

And that's not to suggest that dating through the personals has been without its share of incidents. In our interviewing, we came across people who've met unsavory characters and encountered potentially dangerous situations through the personals.

Remember Sally from Chapter 1? She recognized an ad in the paper as one that she had answered months earlier, so she decided to try again, explained that she had previously responded to one of his ads, and requested a phone conversation. This time the guy did call back and they discovered that they were both members of the same organization. "I'd felt a bond then," she said. "So I let my guard down." She told him more details about herself. But a face-to-face date never happened. Rather, he started making obscene phone calls to her, showing up at her office, stalking her. So what did she do? She went to the police, had her phone tapped, and reported the incidents along with the box number to the publication that ran his ad, discovering in the process that there were 10 other complaints against this man. She threatened legal action against the publication unless they could get him to stop harassing and stalking her. They did. And she hasn't heard from the man again.

Peter, from chapters 2 and 7, also experienced a stalking situation early in his use of the personals. It started when Margaret responded to an ad that he'd placed. But while they had long—and enjoyable—phone conversations, they were unable to meet because she was going out of town for a month. They talked regularly during this time and he had high hopes for the relationship. On her return, he picked her up at the airport, they went out to dinner, and she spent the night at his apartment.

The next morning, he started having reservations. Her statements were inconsistent and lacking in specifics. And he felt that she had physically misrepresented herself. "If she had been up front, it wouldn't have been a problem," he said. "But the fact that she tried to hide it and wasn't comfortable with it was a problem." He felt that she had low self-esteem. He decided to break off the relationship before it went any further. "I got this spooky feeling from her," he said. "We went for a walk and I said that it wasn't working. She was upset."

He thought he was done with her. A couple of weeks later, however, she started stalking him, leaving obscene phone messages, pulling up alongside him in a car while he was out running, laying on her car horn in the middle of the night outside his apartment building. When she saw that he seemed unfazed by this harassment, she stopped. And this experience did not stop Peter from using personal ads again, explaining that "it's as easy to meet unstable people in a bar as it is through the mail."

Of course, in today's violent world, Peter is correct; meeting new people under any circumstances is risky. The world is filled with cons, unfaithful spouses, and hoards of men and women with addictions and violent inclinations. If you're meeting a lot of new people, you're bound to have a few unsavory characters cross your path. This can happen anywhere—at work, in church, or through friends.

But is it any more dangerous to date through the personals? To find out, we asked J. J. Bittenbinder, a national expert and speaker on personal safety. He is a 20-year veteran of the Chicago Police Department, where he spent 17 years as a detective in the homicide and violent crimes division. During his career, he has interviewed more than 1,000 victims, witnesses, and offenders involved in violent crime. He has since emerged as one of America's leading experts on crime and personal security and currently serves as the crime prevention expert on *Good Morning America.* In addition, he makes numerous appearances on local and national radio and television programs, including *The Oprah Winfrey Show* and *ABC News,* and is the author of *Tough Target: A Street-Smart Guide to Staying Safe.*

"It's not *how* people meet," Bittenbinder told us. "It's what happens after they meet." And he recommends that security precautions start right away. So what should you do? "There are no absolutes. Use *your* judgment. I'm not going to be so pedantic as to say you have to meet this guy five times before you take him to your house. I just really believe that you have to be a little cautious and check this guy out."

But while Bittenbinder never dated through the personals, he has some savvy advice for playing it smart: "You can do anything you want on the phone and anything you want through the mail because those things—the mailboxes—are anonymous." But, once things get a little more personal, a few safety precautions are necessary. Specifically, Bittenbinder recommends the following.

- Don't give your home phone number right off—at least not until you can look into his or her face—and get a feel for this individual.
- Meet in a public place, like a bar or a restaurant; then go to a public event like a sporting event or a concert—somewhere where there are lots of people.
- Provide your own transportation to the meeting and then back home.
- At the end of the date, make sure that you're not being followed home.
- If you don't like the person, don't give him or her your home phone number—or the right phone number, if this individual persists in getting one.

"Not only does this [advice] work for a [newspaper] personal ad," he says, "it works for meeting someone on-line." Here are some more words of advice from Bittenbinder.

Don't Rely on Dating-Service Background Checks

"You cannot rely on personal ads—and especially dating services— who say that they run complete checks on people," he warns. "They take a lot [of information] on face value. If this guy says that his name is John F. Kennedy, they may run John F. Kennedy and find out that he's clear, but when we get this guy back in the saddle, we may find his name is actually Gerald Ford. So don't be fooled by people who say they run complete name checks."

Don't Let Your Date See Your Car

"You can learn a lot from an automobile—even if you don't run a license plate," he warns. "You're giving away a lot of information. If you have a parking sticker from a college or a residential building, or even a city sticker, then this guy knows where you live. I don't even recommend that she park in a nearby space where he can go out and look at her car. Rather, I would park away from this guy, walk away, and that's it."

Pay Attention

"Look for lies. If the guy says he's not a drinker and he comes with liquor on his breath then you know he's a liar. Look at this guy and remember what he said. And if he said something different, did it change or did he lie? Or which time did he lie? Get rid of this goof. You'll save yourself a lot of problems."

Come Prepared

"She should have all the things that she needs. She should have her purse with her and she might even bring pepper spray. I'm not saying she has to worry about spraying this guy, but you don't know if he's going to be able to take care of her either. And if he doesn't take care of her, then she has to take care of herself. And she should be ready to do that. I'd rather see her prepared with that pepper spray and not need it, than need it and not have it."

Don't Let Your Date Drive You Home

Bittenbinder recommends a little caution when considering taking public transportation to a date. "The thing to avoid is getting into a situation where it's cold outside or raining and he says, 'I'll drive you home, so you don't have to wait for the bus' and she looks like a jerk if she says no. I don't think that she should let him drive her to and from the date."

Don't Offer to Drive Your Date Home

"If he took public transportation and she took her car, then does that mean she is supposed to drive him home? No. Go home alone. Give him the ground rules. I just really believe that you have to be a little cautious."

Trust Your Gut

"If you've got a feeling that there is something wrong, then there is something wrong. And you should go with that feeling. Don't start thinking with your heart. Say you've got a young daughter and you look at this goofy guy who comes to pick her up and you really know in your heart that this guy is not good, but your daughter says, 'But, Mom, I love him; he's so good to me.' She's not thinking right. Don't be blinded by love. You have to look through the candy and flowers to the person who's holding them. You have to understand that this guy has goals, needs, and wants. Find out what he was doing before he met you and try to understand his motivation."

Check Them Out

"There are a lot of ways to check guys out. You can see if he's ever been in prison. You can check his credit with the social security number on his driver's license. A private investigator can run a name check on the guy—for a couple hundred bucks. All you need is a social security number and date of birth or a license plate number."

Get to Know Him

"She should want to go where *he* works. See where *he* lives. Meet *his* friends." If you can't go to his workplace, Bittenbinder suggests that you "call up the employer and say, 'My name is Maryann. We're a florist three blocks down and we've got flowers for so-and-so and what department does he work in so we can have our guy drop these off. No? You don't have anyone there by that name?'" That, according to Bittenbinder, would help verify employment—and the individual's honesty level.

Don't Assume That Anyone Is Harmless or Honest

"People don't come down the street with a swastika in the middle of their foreheads like Charles Manson has," Bittenbinder says half jokingly. "These people look like nice guys. A lot of these people on the Internet are wonderful, but there are a few who try to scam. At first, he's a charming guy. Next thing you know he needs a little bit of money because one of his horses is sick and he says, 'Could you lend me about $500?' You know, as soon as he asks for money, the red flag should come up and you should say, 'Whoa.' I would not recommend anyone lending—or giving—money for any reason at all in the early part of a relationship. It just isn't smart."

Warning: Don't Be a Different Type of Target

In giving this advice, Bittenbinder directs his comments mostly toward women, because they have been the recipients of most of the scams. "It usually is the man conning the woman," he says. "In my book *Tough Target: A Street-Smart Guide to Staying Safe,* there's a story of this guy who has been married 83 times. He would just marry them, take their money, and then run away. And they finally caught him and now he's in jail." Bittenbinder pointed out that scams like this one happen all the time, but "most of these stories don't make the news."

He also says that his advice is applicable to men, but they tend to ignore him. "They don't believe that they're vulnerable. They're macho," he says. "They block it out as fast as they block out commercials for feminine products." But men aren't safe from deception. In fact, that's the lesson Ron learned. An extremely successful business owner in Tucson, he avoided disaster by maintaining a healthy level of skepticism. He had sent a letter to a woman he'd seen a photo of in a singles magazine, claiming that she was one of the most beautiful women he had ever seen. Naturally, Ron emphasized his fortune and comfortable lifestyle. "I'm a salesman," he said. "Like any product, I was just trying to present the best benefits I could offer."

Nikki wrote him back saying that he was everything she needed in life. She was out of work and needed a new start. If he treated her to the life that he described, then it would be the best thing that could ever happen to her and she'd be eternally grateful.

They talked on the phone after that. They seemed compatible. They had common interests. Everything was falling into place and Nikki was almost ready to make the move. There was just one thing: She lived with a physcially handicapped roommate who was just like a sister to her. This woman needed $425 to cover her share of the rent for the month . . . in cash . . . sent to a P.O. box.

It wasn't the money that concerned Ron. What bothered him was the fact that she'd asked him so early in their relationship. So Ron decided to call the police in Nikki's town. His story sparked their interest. Apparently, she regularly seduced conventioneers, married men, clergy, and other men who valued discretion. After taking photos of them in compromising positions, she blackmailed them. Her scams netted her about $80,000 a year. They staked out her P.O. box and arrested her.

The lesson? If something about an ad—or any follow-up conversation—makes you uneasy, use it as a warning sign. Report it or ignore it, but whatever you do, don't be a target for crime. Because while we suggested that personal-ad users target their message and their media choices, we don't want you to be involved with this type of targeting. So, in addition to Bittenbinder's advice, here are some suggestions given by the personal-ad users that we interviewed.

Don't Rent a P.O. Box at the Post Office

Because the post office is a government entity, any citizen has a right to information about post office transactions. So renting a P.O. box there doesn't guarantee anonymity. To maintain privacy, opt for the mailboxes owned and operated by the publication or rent one from a company like Mail Boxes, Etc. or Kinko's. It may cost a little more, but it will pay off in the added safety and security.

Keep—and Use—Your Records

While we've already recommended keeping a log in previous chapters, we can't stress the importance of this enough. One person we interviewed started keeping a log because she found it impossible to remember all the men who sent her "instant messages" during chat sessions over the Internet. From this log, she was able to discover that many men were using multiple screen names, enabling her to weed out people who were trying to be deceptive.

Leave a Trail

If you're going out with someone for the first time, let a friend or family member know where you're going, when you'll be back, and who you're with. Tell them you're going out with someone you don't know very well and give them your date's name, phone number, and any other information that you may have. During your first date, you can get a license plate number and leave it (along with his name and a description of his car) on a friend's answering machine.

Don't Take Caution Personally

While we're telling you to be cautious, you should also recognize that your date may be doing this as well. If he doesn't want you to see his car, find a place where both of you can meet and not travel. If he wants to meet your friends, accept that this is part of his selection process. Eventually both of you will have to reveal more information, but you should be understanding—and aware —of this process.

Don't Negotiate

Gavin De Becker, in his book *The Gift of Fear,* warned that "when a woman gets 30 messages from a pursuer and doesn't call him back, but then finally gives in and returns his calls, no matter what she says, he learns that the cost of reaching her is 30 calls." De Becker's advice? Cut all ties. And explicitly state the rejection. "Any connection after a rejection will be seen as negotiation." And the man might then try to show why he's right for her, which can evolve into stalking.

A Final Cautionary Tale

Fresh out of a long marriage, Joe would get together with Liz at a little club near her house. He was hungry for romance and knew that he'd eventually go home with her, but he was willing to wait a while until they got to know a little about each other first. But after a few dates, he found himself in her apartment. And they quickly moved into her bedroom. With their foreplay, he was more than ready. However, whenever he made a move, she delayed the act. An intermission. A question or a comment. Then their foreplay would resume until he again would make a move. And then another interruption. This continued for several hours.

Joe hadn't had enough one-night stands to know if this was unusual, but he did know that he couldn't stand it any longer. With her approach taking its toll, he decided that a good night's sleep in his own bed might be the better option. So he left. And she followed, traveling behind him all the way to where he parked his car on a busy street. There, as a final gesture, she lifted her blouse and exposed her breasts to her would-be lover, letting him see what he'd be missing.

"I just bolted," he said. His conclusion: "There are a lot of weird people out there." So keep that in mind when you date. Proceed. But proceed with caution.

10

Cindy Crawford *Meets* Don Knotts

Too many people miss the silver lining because they're expecting gold.

—*Maurice Sitter*

After going on a large number of dead-end dates, Rachel decided to try the personals. "It couldn't be worse," she said, by way of explaining her decision. At first she considered answering an ad or two, but felt that placing one would give her more control. She chose the *Houston Press,* a liberal weekly arts-oriented newspaper in her community. While she didn't keep the ad, she recalled that it included the following information as well as the age range of the man that she wanted to meet:

> SWF, 28, liberal teacher. Looking for someone interested in books, long walks, and talking.

She then explained on her voice-mail message that she taught school and also gave more details on her background and interests. Rachel got more than 25 responses—many of them were from doctors and lawyers. "I found that refreshing," she said, "and it showed me that this was OK to do."

She followed up on four of the voice-mail responses. She dated one guy three or four times; another, just once. The third guy canceled before she even met him. And the fourth was Ron. He said that he hated Texas, was only there for a job, and had gone to graduate school in the East. (The same university—it turned out—that she had attended for her graduate degree. And, coincidentally, she was there at the same time as Ron.)

Like Rachel, he described himself as being "liberal," which she found intriguing. And she liked his accent.

Ron left his voice-mail response during the last week in April, but she didn't call him back until the first week in June. They played phone tag. But, finally, they connected, talked several times over the phone, and then arranged to meet for dinner at a popular Mexican restaurant. After dinner, they drove in separate cars to a bar to continue their date. The tone of their conversation changed when they went to the bar: from chatty and light during dinner to topics that were more serious in nature.

There was just one problem: she didn't like him much because she felt that he was trying too hard to impress her. But since she appreciated that they were both concerned about the same issues, she agreed to go on a second date with him. This one went much better—he didn't try as hard to impress her—so she agreed to see him a third time. This date also went well. They continued dating, and three months after they first met, they started talking about marriage. They were formally engaged three months after that. And shortly after their third wedding anniversary, Rachel gave birth to a healthy baby girl.

Like Rachel, you may have placed your ad, gotten a lot of responses, and talked to a few of them. The voice-mail messages sounded great. The phone conversations also went well. You're excited. Optimistic. Perhaps even a little stunned that an ad can actually bring someone into your life who you're interested in meeting.

Then it hits you: you have to go on a date. Sure, you've been on dates before—even blind dates. You debate your strategy. You realize that in many ways, it's like a traditional date. You want to connect. You want to have fun. And you want a little romance. In other ways, it's different. The first date through an ad is a continuation of the selection process that we described in Chapter 8. Your goal is to learn more about the other person, validate the information you've already gathered on the phone to see if there are any inconsistencies, and decide if—and why—you should continue seeing each other.

Remember, even with this goal, a good date won't just happen. You have to plan for it. Be specific. Clarify the details. Decide ahead of time on all of the who, what, where, when, and how questions. That means you need to answer the following questions before your date.

- Who will be there? Are you—or is the other person—going to bring a friend? People do this all the time, both as a safety measure and as an insurance policy in the event the date turns out to be a dud. And it's OK—if the other person knows beforehand. Otherwise, the date might feel insulted. So don't let it be a surprise.

- What are you going to do? If you're meeting at a restaurant, will it be for a meal or just for coffee? A full meal may give you more time to get to know the other individual, but coffee alone gives both parties a quicker way out—and less financial investment—if the date is a dud. Either way is fine depending on your comfort level, but when one person eats and the other just orders coffee, the date can get awkward, with the sipper doing most of the talking because the diner's mouth is full. This same consideration holds for dates in other places. Your goal should be to avoid any awkward situations for either individual.

- Where will you meet? And do you have the address? Then once you get there, will you wait for your date outside or inside the location? If you're planning to meet outside, what will you do if it rains? If you're going to be inside, where? By the front door? A side door? At a booth or a table? Since you really don't know the person you're meeting, getting firm answers to all of these questions becomes even more important, because if you get your signals crossed—or fear that you might—there's no way to identify the other person.

- When will you meet? Again, specifics are important, so be sure to confirm the exact day and time. Negotiate how long the date will last. If you have to leave to pick up a child or attend a meeting, let the other person know in advance, so he or she won't be offended when you leave.

- How will you recognize each other? This is one of the most important questions for you to get answered up front. What will you be wearing? What about your date? Describe any unique features you have. Ask your date to do the same. Remember, in all likelihood, you're going to be meeting your date in a crowded public place. There may be other people waiting to meet someone they've never met. They may even be wondering if you're their date. You don't want to have to approach them to find the person you're expecting to meet.

Without addressing these specific points, your date may never happen. And while these questions may seem obvious, when you're nervously setting up—or getting ready for—a date, they're easily forgotten.

What's more, you should never assume your date understands the plan. You can save yourself—and your date—a lot of worry and embarrassment by making detailed plans.

But it's not just the logistical questions that need to be addressed. Your dating style and strategy should also be clear up front. For instance, do you, like John from Chapter 6 or Sally from Chapter 1, prefer to meet people at a coffee house and screen them before going on full-fledged dates with them? Or do you prefer to screen people more fully on the phone—like George from Chapter 6—and then jump into some activity? Or do you not even want to screen people; rather, you just meet them for some activity? While there are no right or wrong answers, the following considerations can help you identify your personal-ad dating styles and strategies.

Go to It

It's not uncommon for people who use the personals to be stood up. Some interviewees feel that their dates actually do show up, but don't introduce themselves; rather, they vanish when they're not interested. We've been unable to determine which happens more often. But other people have left during a date. Remember Erica? She had dazzled Ed with the response package we described in Chapter 7. But he arrived a half hour late for their date at a popular downtown restaurant. And then when Erica excused herself to go to the ladies room, he left. That's right. In the five minutes that she took to go to the ladies room, he vanished. But don't feel sorry for her. Two men at the bar, who'd been observing the situation, came to console her. She spent a long time talking with them and they took her out dancing. She had a great evening.

Brew Up Some Romance

Many first dates take place in a coffee shop over a steamy mocha—which is slightly strange when you consider that dating through an ad is like a blind date and most blind dates don't occur in coffee shops. Most blind dates that are set up by friends or relatives usually consist of one person taking another to a movie, dinner, bowling, a concert, or anywhere else dating couples tend to go.

What's the difference? Many personal-ad users we interviewed didn't think of their first meeting as a date. To them, the event was more like a mutual, in-person job interview—which makes the coffee shop, in essence, the romantic employment office of the '90s. It's just a follow-up step in the selection process, a continuation of the phone conversation. It's where the two people ask probing questions, get a feeling for each other, see if the facts check out, and determine if they want to spend more time together.

Like anything else, meeting for coffee has its advantages and disadvantages. This is a low-investment activity. You don't need a lot of money or a credit card. You can learn a lot about your date by just talking. You're in a public place, so it's safe. And you can do it at any time of the day, so it can even fit into the most rigid of schedules. Plus, it's a culturally neutral and universal activity. If your date doesn't show, you can still enjoy it by yourself. And it's trendy.

On the other hand, meeting for coffee—or dinner or drinks, for that matter—can put enormous pressure on each person to make quick decisions about the other. Do you like him or her? Are you physically attracted to this person? Would you be interested in spending more time with this individual? What does your gut say about him or her? You ask yourself all these questions because your focus is on determining your next step and helping your date determine whether he or she wants to spend more time with you not on enjoying the here and now.

That's the major disadvantage of having coffee, a drink, or a dinner date; you may find it difficult to establish a comfortable foundation for further contact when coffee or a meal is the only experience that you've shared. So if you choose to meet for coffee and you'd like to see the person again, try to identify a common interest that would take the pressure off developing a romance. Make your decisions based on your need for a good tennis partner, a shared interest in classic films, or some other mutual interest. That way you will feel less pressure to develop a relationship right away. You'll have time to get to know the person and become friends. Then a relationship may form naturally.

Decaffeinate Your Dates

So if you've decided not to grab coffee—or you need a quick idea for a second date—where should you go to meet? Cyndi Haynes and Dale Edwards offer quite a few creative and fun ideas in their book *2002 Things to Do on a Date.* When selecting ideas, however, make sure that you evaluate them in light of the safety considerations we presented in Chapter 9. To get you started, here are some ideas that can leave you with more than a conversation. After reading this list, see if you can come up with a few ideas of your own.

- Meet at a movie, play, or concert; then discuss it over coffee to see if both of you are on the same wavelength.
- Volunteer with your date at an animal shelter, museum, hospital, etc. Doing good for society can do good for your love life when you have a chance to bond with your date.
- Attend a museum exhibit; then each of you will be able to see how the other one interprets the world.
- Meet at a flea market or go shopping. This will give each of you a chance to discuss your personal style.
- Meet at a sporting event. Rooting for the same team or sharing the feeling of victory —or defeat—can do more to form a bond than a coffee house grind can.
- Register for the same class—anything from horseback riding to pottery to modern literature.
- Meet at a boat, car, home, or other trade show. Here you'll discover the kind of big-ticket items you and your date want to own.
- Browse through a bookstore or library. You'll be able to see if you have common interests. And there's nothing better than discussing a good book.

- Attend a political event. After all, everything in life is, in essence, political, so this will give you a chance to see if you have the same political style and outlook on life. You'll also see how you handle the differences.
- Work out at a health club. Healthy competition can lead to a healthy romance, so do not overlook sweating with your potential Mr. or Ms. Right.

In choosing an activity, pick something you would like to do anyway. Or consider something that you've been wanting to do but prefer to experience with another person. That way, you've accomplished something. And, we hope, you've had a good time in the process.

Start Talking

Because of the element of anonymity in playing the personals, you can be more inquisitive, open, and direct than when you meet someone through traditional channels. This means that you can get to know each other more quickly—perfect because, as we already mentioned, this is when you need to form a bond with your date.

As with any first date, you have an infinite number of topics that you can discuss. Some are obvious: how you and your date feel about using the personals and your history (as well as your date's history) with them. This can allow you to explore past relationships, reasons for breakups, and views on commitment and dating. Some topics are less obvious: what you or your date was like as a child; where you or your date likes to go for vacations—and why. Topics such as these allow each of you to communicate your personality and show how you think.

To get the most out of your conversation with your date, ask open-ended questions, because the how and the why of something calls for more than a yes or a no answer. For instance, you can ask your date why he or she responded to your ad and what he or she found important or intriguing in it. When listening to the answer, ask yourself if his or her response makes sense. See if your date tends to blame former partners for his or her failed relationships. Once or twice may be OK, but not every time. After all, he or she did play a part in those relationships and should have some accountability for the results.

When listening, be sure to see whether his or her answers are specific or vague. If a comment creates a negative or ambiguous picture, ask for clarification. If your date responds with a defensive, evasive answer, consider this a red flag. Sure, it could be that your date is just nervous, but it could also be that he or she is lying. Since your date should want you to know more about himself or herself, your request for clarification could either help move the conversation along or signal to you that this person is trying to hide something.

Don't Be Afraid to Open Up and Connect

Shawn, whom we introduced in Chapter 4, said this—and he's right. At this early stage, it's important to discover a potential partner's willingness to communicate—as important, in fact, as the content of that communication. In addition, if you feel comfortable discussing a certain subject, you should. If your date is shocked, turned off, or intimidated by your openness or candor, you might not be right for each other. But if your date is interested, you may have found your match.

Make Sure Your Conversation Is Balanced

Don't be the one to ask all the questions. And don't monopolize the conversation. This point may seem obvious to you, but because of nerves, it is often forgotten. What's more, we found that people in some professions may be more or less likely to talk about themselves. For example, Jan expected Tim to be more adept at having a healthy relationship and more understanding and communicative because he was a psychologist. But on their date, he reverted to his professional role. He asked one question after another about her background, family, and past relationships. And he rarely revealed his own feelings, responding instead with noncommittal nods. She left the lunch feeling as though she'd been psychoanalyzed and never called him again.

Be Careful with What You Reveal

Someday, your date may be part of your life. He or she may get to know your close friends, parents, and employer. So while the initial anonymity of the date through the personals may make you comfortable with revealing very private information, imagine how you'll feel down the road knowing that he or she has this intimate knowledge of you. This is not to say that you should be dishonest. Just keep private the facts that won't affect a potential relationship with that individual.

Share the Big Issues in Your Life

While we've warned against revealing too much, you should put issues that will affect your relationship on the table as soon as possible. Are you caring for an aging parent? Do you suffer from herpes? Are you waiting for your divorce to be finalized? These are points you should communicate to your potential partner, because they'll play a role in the dynamics of your relationship. You don't have to make it a big issue. Just let the conversation guide you to a point where you say to yourself, "*Now* it's time to tell him or her that I've been in AA for five years." Then say it. Share the events that created the situation and how your other partners have handled it. Show why it should be a nonissue for your prospective partner. If he or she finds your situation to be a stumbling block for a relationship between the two of you, then you've saved time and heartache by ending it early on.

Be Prepared for Coincidences

It's not unusual for two people who meet through the personals to already have a common connection. Remember Peter and Claira from earlier chapters? They had mutual friends and played volleyball at the same club. Rachel and Ron from the start of this chapter had attended the same university at the same time—years before they had met each other. When Sandy met Anthony through the personals, she learned that he was a longtime friend of her boss's family. Fortunately, they were both self-conscious about meeting through the personals, so neither of them ever acknowledged the source of their friendship to their common connection.

Limit Your Time

When you're going to meet a person for the first time, limit the amount of time that you'll spend with him or her. Susan Page, author of *If I'm So Wonderful Why Am I Still Single?*, suggests limiting a first meeting to two hours or less. If you're simply meeting to talk over coffee, two hours will provide you with enough time to get to know the other person and to set up your next date. If the date is boring, it's a short enough time to politely endure and still not waste your entire evening. And if the date is going so well that you lose track of time, your limit wouldn't matter anyway.

Manage Expectations

Many people we interviewed said that when they expressed an interest in seeing a date again, the date's expectation level soared beyond their comfort level. They began to wonder: "Will he or she expect me to call for a date this Saturday? Then the following Saturday? Then every Friday and Saturday after that?"

When this happens, many people just walk away rather than plan further dates because they are unsure whether the rewards will be worth the risks. Consequently, these dates ended up being nice evenings—and lost opportunities.

To keep this from happening, let your date know what you expect when you ask for another date or express an interest in taking the relationship further. If you want to go slow—and you probably should when you don't know the person too well—say that. Just like in business, this task—letting the other person know what to expect—is an important key to building relationships.

Unfortunately, there's no good way to learn to use this skill except by trial and error. So you should develop and then practice the skills of managing expectations as much as you work on refining your ad. It'll pay off in all aspects of your life.

Have Fun

So far, all of this advice may make a first date through the personals sound far too serious. But don't forget to have a good time. It should be enjoyable. Talk about what excites you: your children, your family, your last vacation, your work, current events. And do things that you want to do. After all, that's part of why you're dating. If you're not enjoying the experience you may as well just stay at home.

Ask for Feedback

At the end of your date, you should decide if you want to meet again. This doesn't mean that you have to decide if you want a permanent relationship (as a friend or a lover)—just a second date. So ask your date if he or she had an enjoyable time. See how he or she would like your date to be different the next time.

If your date doesn't want to see you again, ask why (while assuring him or her that you're not trying to create an argument; that you'd just appreciate the information for future reference). Chances are, you'll find that the reason isn't so much a matter of desirability, but one of compatibility.

If you hear something negative, don't be offended. Rather, appreciate that your date had the courage to be frank—and take the feedback for what it's worth. It can help on your next date with someone else. And remember, one of the best aspects of dating through the personals is that there's always another opportunity.

Be Tough

We have found that since dates through the personals are anonymous—no common friends or family members to answer to—some people are inclined to be cruel. They're harsh with criticism or late in arriving. So be prepared to toughen up a bit. And even though we just suggested that you also ask for feedback, keep your ego intact. Just keep looking for your perfect match. And remember, the insensitive actions of others are not a reflection of you—only a reflection of them.

Accept Rejection Graciously

No one enjoys it, but if you're playing the personals, rejection is inevitable. Fortunately, this usually happens before you've invested much time or effort into the new relationship. So don't feel devastated by it. Just go back to your log of responses—or answer a few more ads. And, remember, even the hottest movie stars endured rejection at some point in their lives. It didn't stop them. And it shouldn't stop you.

Respect the Word *No*

Everyone has a right to say no. Respect that. Being on the receiving end of a rejection doesn't make you less desirable to other people. So just move on. You always have other opportunities—that's the beauty of the personals. And as we've stated, rejection is usually a sign of perceived incompatibility, not a measure of your attractiveness.

Wait to Find Out If You're Actually Being Rejected

Sometimes big issues or incidents in a person's life may interfere with his or her ability to follow up right away on the date. That's just what happened to Peter. Right before he met Claira, he met Joyce through the personals. They had a great date, discovered that they had a lot in common, and agreed that they should see each other again. So, as they discussed, he kept his next weekend open. She'd promised to call to finalize the arrangements, which he respected. So he didn't call her. Rather, he waited by the phone. Thursday, no call; Friday, nothing again. Of course, he also didn't hear from her on Saturday or Sunday. His weekend was shot. On Monday, he decided to leave a scathing message on her answering machine. "I thought we had a good time," he said. "At least, you could have called. Then I wouldn't have waited for you." A few days later she called back and said that she had been called out of town because her grandfather had died; she had planned to get back to him but didn't because the events were too overwhelming. Because of his message, she requested that he never call her again.

Trust Your Gut

You intuition is usually right. So pay attention to it. But this does not mean heeding rational advice because it sounds right or "healthy"—or yielding to your heart's lust. Trusting your gut is listening to what your body is saying. For example, let's say you're on a date. He or she is average looking. There's nothing about the appearance that you'd identify as sinister. You've chosen to meet in a crowded restaurant, clearly a safe environment. Yet you don't feel safe. Don't try to tell yourself that it's just your nerves. It's not. Your gut is trying to tell you something, so listen to it. It's better to be safe than sorry.

Deliver Rejection with Kindness

So you're sitting across a table from your date and after his or her fourth cigarette in the last half hour, you realize that it's important that your partner be a nonsmoker. Funny, since you didn't even think to ask if he or she smoked. But now you're ready for an oxygen tent and you haven't even finished your coffee. This is a typical—though exaggerated—story of what happens when dating through the personals. Use this experience as a way of further defining your needs and refining your expectations.

When you find that you're lacking chemistry with your date, just say so. And don't get personal or criticize. The sooner you do this, the better. Then there's less invested in the relationship—and less let-down. Your date may even feel the same way and appreciate the fact that you spoke up first. Verbalize your feelings. But couch it around your needs, not his or her shortcomings.

If you find the person has qualities you definitely don't want—such as dishonesty, a bad temper, or an addiction—be direct. Tell him or her that you find certain behavior unacceptable and that you are not inter-ested in pursuing a relationship. Don't be steered into negotiating. And don't waste any more of your time. Just bring the date to an end quickly but graciously.

Explore the Possibilities of Friendship

You never know what can come from a date. When you're direct with your assessment of a relationship's possibilities, you may have an opportunity to cultivate other possibilities. Just be open to them. Maybe you've found your next employer. A sister or brother-in-law. Or a new friend. Remember Ann from Chapter 4? She connected with Bob, a pilot, but found that they really didn't have enough in common to build a romance. They did share enough to form a friendship, how-ever, and now he's helping her study for a pilot's license.

Remember That a Bad Date Can Be a Good Experience

Pay attention and you can learn a lot on a bad date. For instance, it can help you identify the qualities you don't want in a special some-one. And it can help you rearrange your priorities and point you toward possibilities that you'd have never imagined. If your date is rude to you, don't take it personally. Just think: You will never have to see that person again, so consider yourself lucky.

Pay Your Own Way

Since the '60s, dating has been plagued with one big economic ques-tion: Who should pay for the date? There are many ways to determine the answer. Who placed the ad? Who asked whom for the date? Who earns more? How will the man feel if the woman pays? How will the woman feel if the man takes her up on her offer to pay? How will the woman feel if the man doesn't pay? To eliminate this dilemma, we're going make it really simple and declare once and for all that each per-son should pay his or her own way on the first meeting through a personal ad. Both of you agreed to meet. You should both have under-stood the cost. On subsequent dates, you and your partner can deter-mine who pays any way you'd like. But on a first meeting—when very little has been invested emotionally and you're just getting together to see if you want to date—splitting the bill is the best way to go. Then you and your date won't feel obligated to each other in any way.

Make Fear Your Friend

Fear is a wonderful motivator. If you're nervous about meeting your date, use your fear to motivate you to look your best, feel your best, and plan for safety. And then when you've found someone you con-sider important in your life, use the fear of losing that opportunity to motivate you to pursue it.

True Love: More than a Question of Chemistry

When the chemistry is right, it's easy to think that a relationship has more potential than it may actually have. You see the fireworks. You hear the music. You feel great. That's how Colleen felt when she first kissed Gor-dan, a divorced marketing director with custody of three sons.

When she met him on-line, he seemed flirtatious and fun. And since they both lived in the same area, they met for lunch and made tentative plans to see a movie together on the weekend. He kissed her good-bye and sparks flew. They continued to e-mail each other and met for a romantic lunch at an elegant restaurant later that same week. They held hands under the table. They shared stories about their chil-dren and their divorces. They talked about their jobs. And then, while parting in the parking lot, they kissed so passionately that a Cadillac full of elderly women whistled at them while driving by. They made definite plans to meet again.

Colleen was in heaven—finally, someone with a similar back-ground, someone who was handsome, successful, and passionate.

While driving back to her office, she was on cloud nine. Then a very tiny bird landed on the street in front of her. And it was too late to stop. She careened to the right, but not far enough. She felt the car go over a small mound—one that seemed no bigger than a wad of tissues. She looked into the rearview mirror and saw the remnants of the bird flattened on the tar.

Colleen was so up about her date that she didn't feel remorse. She even noted surprise at her own callousness and thought she'd probably pay for it later in some cosmic way. But her mind was still lip-locked in the parking lot. She imagined all of the wonderful possibilities.

That night she went out with her girlfriend. She parked downtown on a busy street and went into a bar for a few hours. When she returned, her car was gone. The tow zone sign said, "No Parking 6 P.M. to 6 A.M." Unfortunately, still on a cloud from her afternoon lunch, she'd thought it'd read, "No Parking 6 A.M. to 6 P.M." After a frustrating visit to the towing company and a $125 fine, she was back in her car calculating the probable value of a little bird to the cosmos. A few weeks later, her romance with Gordan fizzled.

About a year later, Colleen became romantically involved with Ross, someone who had been a friend of hers for several years. They had great rapport, similar backgrounds, and the same sense of humor. Three hours with Ross seemed to fly by. Having a lot of common interests, they regularly met for lunch. On one particular day, she'd had an especially wonderful time. Driving home she felt satisfied, understood, peaceful—even loved. She was happy.

This time it was a squirrel. The critter darted out in front of her car. She swerved to avoid it. But while she moved left, it moved right and failed to escape the 13-inch Goodyear tire. Colleen looked back and saw the roadkill that she'd just created. Her heart jumped to her throat. Remorse filled her entire being. This time she felt the tragedy.

By the next stop sign, she'd had a revelation. She knew that she cared more deeply for Ross than she had ever cared for Gordan—yet her feelings didn't obliterate her other emotions. She wasn't consumed by them. She wasn't delirious over romance. She didn't have blinders on about Ross's true character. And while she wasn't sure where their relationship would go, she knew that her love for Ross was real.

This story is a great example of how we can get caught up in the frills of dating. It's like going to the mall on a hot summer day for something you really need and forgetting to get it because you're basking in the air conditioning. Everyone wants to feel a little romance and a little passion. But that's not necessarily enough to form the basis of a true, lasting love.

For some people, it takes more than one date to start seeing the desirable qualities of the other individual. For Laura, it took three dates before she started to feel attracted to Tim. She'd placed an ad and received seven responses. She picked her favorite one and spoke with him on the phone a few times before meeting. He seemed nice enough, but nothing clicked. She agreed to see him again, remembering that it was her ad that he'd chosen to answer. And he was her choice from her batch of letters. On the third date, he loosened up and showed his humorous, playful side and she was swept off her feet. They married a few months later.

This situation is typical. People are complex and it takes time to get to know them. Sometimes sparks come later. Without negating the value of physical attraction, Barbara DeAngelis wrote in her book *Are You the One for Me?* that "if you meet someone and aren't immediately attracted to them, it doesn't mean you won't become attracted to them as you get to know them better . . . gradual attraction may be more genuine than "lust at first sight." Additionally, Neil Clark Warren wrote in *Finding the Love of Your Life* that "some couples feel no exhilarating, romantic feelings early in their relationship. Sometimes the strong emotions absent in the beginning gradually grow as the relationship deepens. Just because friends don't feel passionate love initially doesn't mean the relationship should be permanently written off."

So after your date, ask yourself how much of your reaction had to do with you or your date and how much had to do with the situation. What made the date good or bad? Throughout a first date, the question of whether or not to make a second one will probably be going through your mind. There are two schools of thought on this issue. One, if sparks don't fly, don't waste more time. Just cut your losses. And avoid an unpleasant situation down the road. The second school of thought? Give it one more try. That's what Kathy did.

She hated her first date with Jon. She thought that he was conceited; he'd made her feel stupid and self-conscious. That night at home, she said to herself that she'd never want to see him again. But her intuition wasn't buying into her anger. So when he called again, she decided to give him one more try. They went out to a small Middle Eastern restaurant and talked. She learned that he wasn't conceited, just shy and awkward. She fell in love with him that night and decided that he was the one for her. They dated for nearly six months. Then she moved in with him; they got married one year after that, and have already celebrated their sixth wedding anniversary. And their marriage is still going strong.

So if it was a bad date, but something inside tells you to give it one more try, do it. You never know what could happen. The quiet one could knock you off your feet once he or she has the chance to warm up and get to know you. And the love that develops gradually might just well be longer lasting than one that immediately ignites.

Every Love Story Deserves a Happy Ending

Now that you know about the personals, it's time for you to create a story with a happy ending. After all, you'll never know what could happen when you place an ad unless you try it. For inspiration, just look at the story Carl created. A 27-year-old computer engineer, he found himself floundering in the dating scene. But he didn't really expect to meet anyone except in the usual places: bars, grocery stores, or Laundromats. Place a personal ad? He wasn't that desperate. Yet he watched a coworker go out with a different woman almost every night from ads placed in the personals. By watching his coworker, he learned that not all the people who use the personals are psychotic rejects. So he decided to try it.

He looked at it as his opportunity to write the kind of ad that he had always wanted to see in the personals. Something irreverent and witty. After all, he wasn't taking it all that seriously. Sure it would be nice to find some more women to date, but he didn't expect to find a wife. Yet as he struggled with his words, he realized he'd have to be somewhat straight and honest to make his ad work. He wrote:

> Prefer experiences to possessions? Enjoy camping, bicycling, cooking, ethnic dining, alternative films, live music? Adventurous SWM w/unconventional ideas and Midwestern values seeks self-assured, active SWF with heart bigger than her hair.

His ad attracted 16 responses. He met with three of the women. Amanda was a gorgeous blond. She had a great figure. She was bright. In Carl's mind, a definite 10!

But then came reality. She told him how he reminded her of her ex-husband. And he realized his religious perspectives weren't compatible with her born-again Christian beliefs.

Joy seemed to be a good option. She was from his hometown. They learned that they had friends in common. But their relationship didn't go anywhere.

Heidi left him a message late one night: "I'm just sittin' here with my bottle of vodka," she said, her speech slurred, "and I'm wishin' you were right here with me." Carl was entertained, but not enchanted.

In the past, Debra, a physics grad student, had responded to a few ads and dated a few men from the personals. But she was skeptical of ever finding anyone through an ad—even though two of her friends had met their spouses this way. But Carl's ad caught her attention and she left him a message saying that she "ate low on the food chain."

Carl returned her message and after a phone conversation, they agreed to ride their bikes to a lakeside cafe and meet. This date expanded into the rest of the day, winding up at an outdoor concert. But Debra was still skeptical. She was suspicious of his strange work schedule. But she decided to go with it and see what developed. Three years later, they married. And their wedding invitation, which was mentioned in Chapter 1, inspired Sally—as well as other people—to try the personals.

"It took a while for us to fall in love," said Carl. "But we've based our relationship on common interests. We share a lot. And I think our relationship is much deeper for it."

In many ways, the end of Carl and Debra's story—just like the end of this book—is just the beginning. Loving relationships need to develop, grow, and evolve. That takes work and commitment. But the personals are a great place to start. It's true. You can change your life with the right 25 words—or less.

A Word
Catalog

The more specific you can be, the better. Use the following list to help you identify words for our exercises in Chapters 3 and 4, as well as to help get you started on writing your ad. Use your dictionary and thesaurus to identify even more words. Then, for your ad, take the words that you found and see if you can suggest something even more specific. For instance, with the first word, *abrasive* (if this fits you), you may wish to describe yourself as being "as abrasive as a Brillo pad."

A
abrasive
acceptable
accurate
acrobatic
active
adaptable
addictive
adorable
adult
advanced
adventure
adventurous
afire
aggressive
agile

aglow
agreeable
airhead
alien
alluring
ally
amazing
amiable
amorous
amuse
ancient
android
angel
angelic
angry
animal

animated
antique
antiseptic
appeal
applicant
approachable
appropriate
aristocratic
aromatic
artistic
ascetic
aspiring
astonishing
astounding
athletic
attainable

attentive
attractive
austere
authentic

B
babe
bachelor
bad
baffling
balanced
ballad
ballerina
banned
banquet
barbaric
barefoot
baroque
bashful
basic
beautiful
beauty
belle
beloved
berserk
better
bewitching
biting
bitter
blasé
blast
blatant
blazing
blazon
blended
blissful
bloodcurdling
blunt

boisterous
bold-faced
bombproof
bona fide
bountiful
bouquet
boyish
brainy
brand-new
brave
brawny
brazen
breezy
brief
bright
brilliant
brimming
brisk
brittle
brotherly
bubbly
budding
buttery
buzz

C
calm
caloric
candid
candied
cantankerous
capable
capitalistic
careful
caress
casual
cathartic
catlike

caustic
cautious
cavernous
celebrated
cement
cerebral
certified
chance
changeable
chaotic
character
chaste
chauffeur
cheeky
cherry
cherub
chicken
childish
childproof
chilly
chimerical
chiseled
chivalrous
chock-full
choosy
chummy
circuslike
civil
civilized
clairvoyant
clan
clandestine
classic
classical
clean
clean-cut
clear
clever

clinical
clown
co-ed
coarse
cogent
coherent
cohesive
cold
cold-blooded
colloquial
colonial
color
colorful
colossal
comedian
comfortable
comical
committed
common
commonsensical
compact
companionable
compatible
compelling
competent
competitive
complete
complex
complimentary
comprehensive
compressed
computerized
concentrated
concrete
condensed
confidant
congenial
conscientious

conservative
consistent
contemporary
controlled
controversial
convenient
conventional
convert
cool
correct
correspondent
cosmetic
cosmopolitan
costumed
courageous
courteous
courtly
cowboy
cozy
crackerjack
crave
crazy
creative
credible
creepy
criminal
crucial
cruel
cryptic
curious
customary

D

dainty
dancer
dangerous
dazzle
dazzling

debonair
decadent
deceptive
decisive
declarative
decorative
defrost
delectable
deliberate
delicate
delicious
delight
delightful
delirious
deluge
deluxe
democratic
dependable
dessert
devil
dewy
diabolical
diaphanous
dicey
different
difficult
diffuse
digestible
dignified
diligent
diluted
dinosaur
direct
disciplined
discreet
disposable
disreputable
disrespectful

dissonant
distilled
distinctive
ditto
dog-eared
domestic
dominant
double
downy
dramatic
dreamy
dripping
dry
durable
dynamic
dynasty

E
early
earthy
eastern
easy
easygoing
ebullient
eccentric
economically
edgy
educated
effective
effervescent
efficient
elastic
electric
elegant
elementary
eligible
elite
elusive

emotional
enchanted
encompassing
enduring
engrossing
enigmatic
enormous
enriched
enterprise
entertaining
enthusiastic
enticing
enviable
envisage
episodic
erotic
essential
ethical
ethnic
even
evergreen
everlasting
everyday
evocative
evolutionary
exacting
excellent
excessive
excitable
exclusive
exhaustive
expansive
expedient
expensive
experimental
explicit
explosive
expressive

exquisite
extensive
extraordinary
extrasensory
extravagant
extreme
exuberant

F
fabled
fabulous
facetious
facile
faithful
familiar
famous
fancy
fantastic
fantasy
far-out
far-reaching
fascinate
fashionable
fast
fastidious
father
faultless
favor
feast
featherweight
feathery
feminine
fertile
fervent
fetching
field
fiendish
fierce

fiery
filial
final
finicky
finished
fire
firm
first-class
first-rate
fish
fizzle
flannel
flashy
flat-footed
flavorful
flexible
flimsy
flinty
flippant
flirtatious
float
flowery
fluffy
fluid
fluttery
foamy
focused
fog
folksy
forbidden
forceful
foreign
formal
fragile
fragrant
frank
fraternal
free

fresh
friendly
frightful
frivolous
frolicsome
frontier
frosty
frozen
frugal
fruitful
frustrated
fugitive
full-blooded
full-blown
full-bodied
full-fledged
full-length
full-scale
functional
fundamental
funny
furry

G
gallant
game
gem
generic
generous
genial
gentle
geometric
germ
giddy
gift
gigantic
girlish
glacier

glamorous
glittery
glorious
glossy
gnome
good-natured
gooey
gorgeous
gossamer
graceful
gracious
granitelike
graphic
great
green-eyed
gregarious
gritty
grizzled
guess
gutter

H
habitual
hack
hair-raising
half-wit
hallmark
handsome
happy
hard
hard-boiled
hard-fisted
hardy
harmless
harmonious
harmony
hassle
hawklike

hazardous
hazy
healthful
healthy
hearty
heathen
heavenly
heavy
heavy-duty
heavyweight
helpful
hemisphere
heroic
high-class
high-fidelity
high-spirited
hilarious
historic
hocus-pocus
homegrown
homelike
homespun
homey
honest
honey-eyed
honorable
hopeful
horoscope
hot-blooded
humble
humorous
hungry
hurdle
husky
hybrid
hygienic
hypnotic

I
iconic
icy
ideal
imaginative
immaculate
immense
immodest
immortal
impeccable
impenetrable
imperial
impertinent
impish
import
important
impregnable
impressive
improved
incisive
incomparable
independent
indescribable
indestructible
indirect
indiscreet
indispensable
individual
indomitable
indulgent
ineffable
inexpensive
infallible
infectious
influential
informal
informative
ingenious

innocent
innovative
insidious
instantaneous
intellectual
intense
interchangeable
interesting
interpreter
intimate
intoxicating
intricate
intrigue
intuition
intuitive
invaluable
inventive
investor
investigative
invisible
inviting
ions
ironclad
irrepressible
irresistible
irreverent

J
jaunt
joker
jolly
joy
judicious
junior

K
kangaroo
key

kindhearted
kinetic
king
kitten
knight
knowledgeable

L
labor-saving
lace
ladylike
lamb
languid
lanky
latent
leading
leak-proof
lean
legitimate
leisurely
lengthy
letter-perfect
lifesaving
lighthearted
lightweight
likable
limitless
liquid
literate
little
lived-in
local
loose
lounge
lovable
lovely
lover
low-pressure

lucid
lucky
lucrative
luminous
lurid
luscious
lust
lustrous
lusty
luxurious

M
machinelike
madcap
magnet
magnetic
magnificent
maidenly
majestic
malleable
mammoth
manageable
mandatory
manic
manly
marbleized
martial
marvelous
masculine
mask
match
maternal
mathematical
matronly
matter-of-fact
mature
mechanical
medicinal

medieval
mellow
melodic
memory
mercury
merry
messy
metallic
meteor
method
meticulous
microscopic
middle-aged
Midwestern
might
mild
militaristic
mince
mind
miniature
mink
miracle
mischief
mission
misty
modern
modest
modular
moist
monkey
monumental
moody
moral
motherly
mountainous
mousy
moving
multiform

musical
mutual
mysterious

N
naked
narrow
national
native
natural
naughty
nautical
neat
nebulous
necessary
neighbor
nerdy
nester
night-fly
neutral
new
nice
nimble
nirvana
noble
nocturnal
noisy
nonchalant
nonconformist
normal
noted
noticeable
notorious
nourish
novel
nurturing
nutritious
nutty

O
obedient
objective
obscure
obvious
occultist
octave
odd
off-center
off-key
offbeat
official
oily
old
Olympic
ominous
omnipotent
one-way
opaque
open
optimist
opulent
orchestrate
orderly
ordinary
oriental
original
ornamental
outdoorsman
outrageous
outstanding
oxygen
oyster

P
painless
palatable
palatial

palm
panelist
paradoxical
partner
partier
passionate
patch
paternal
patriot
peaceful
peachy
pearly
peculiar
peer
peerless
peppery
perceptive
perfect
perfumed
perilous
perishable
permanent
permeable
permit
persistent
pervasive
phosphorescent
photogenic
picturesque
pillowy
pinwheel
piquant
pirate
pithy
placid
plain
plastic
playful

pleasant
pleasing
plebeian
plentiful
poem
poetic
poignant
point
pointed
polite
pool
popular
porous
portentous
potent
powdery
power
powerful
practical
praiseworthy
precious
precise
predictable
preferred
pretender
pretty
priceless
pride
primary
prison
private
productive
professional
profound
progressive
prominent
prompt
propeller

proper
prophet
proprietary
protective
proven
proverbial
provincial
provocative
prude
psychic
puff
puffy
pumpkin
punctual
puppyish
pure

Q

quack
qualify
qualm
quasi-
quick
quiet
quilt
quit

R

race
radiant
radical
rag
ragged
rampage
rank
rapturous
rare
rational

rawboned
real
reasonable
recover
red-hot
reel
referee
refined
reflection
refresh
refreshing
regular
reinforce
reject
relaxed
relief
remarkable
removable
Renaissance
render
renew
replaceable
reputable
reserve
reside
resilient
responsible
reversible
revolutionary
reward
rhythmic
rich
ride
right
rigid
rigorous
risky
risqué

roar
roguish
romantic
rooster
rosy
rough
roughhouse
route
routine
rowdy
royal
rugged
rural

S
salty
salute
sandal
saturated
savage
savor
savory
scandal
scanty
scarce
scenic
scholar
scientific
scoop
score
scratch
scream
scrub
scrumptious
scrupulous
seasoned
secretive
secure

sedate
seductive
seed
seeker
self-assured
self-conscious
self-contained
senatorial
senile
sensible
sensual
sentimental
serene
serious
serve
settle
severe
shadowy
shapely
sharp
sheltering
shine
shipper
shiver
shock
shockproof
shoot
short-term
shrewd
sign
significant
silent
silken
silvery
simple
sinful
sinewy
single

sizzle
skilled
skunk
sky-high
sleepy
slip
slippery
slow
smoky
smooth
snarled
snobbish
snowman
snowy
soaking
sober
sociable
solemn
solid
solitary
sonnet
soul
soulful
south
southern
sovereign
spacious
special
spectacular
spell
spice
spider
spirit
spiritual
splendid
spontaneous
spotless
squeaky

squint
stable
stainless
standard
star
starch
starlit
startle
stately
steadfast
sterile
stirring
stocky
streamlined
strident
strong
stud
stupendous
stylish
suave
sublime
submerge
substantial
subtle
suburban
subversive
successful
succulent
sumptuous
sunbaked
sunlit
sunny
superb
superior
supple
supplement
supreme
surefire

surreptitious
suspect
svelte
sweet
sympathy
symphonic
synergistic
systematic

T

taboo
tactful
tailor-made
tangible
target
taste
tasty
taut
tawny
technical
teeter
telepathic
telling
temper
temperate
temporary
tenacious
tender
terrific
territorial
terse
testy
thankful
theatrical
therapy
thirsty
thorny
thoroughbred

thought
thoughtful
thrifty
throaty
throttled
thunder
thunderous
tidy
tightfisted
time-honored
timesaving
tiny
Titan
toasted
toe
tongue
top
topical
total
touch
touching
tough
tractable
trade
transfer
transient
translucent
transparent
trash
traveler
triangular
trickster
triumphant
trooper
true
trustworthy
truthful
tuned

tuned-in
two-way
typical

U
ubiquitous
ugly
ulcerated
ultimate
unadorned
uncompromising
unconventional
understand
understated
unfamiliar
uniform
unite
universal
up-to-date
urban
urbane
urchin
use
usher
utopia

V
valley
valuable
vary
vault
vegetable
venerable
Venus
verbal
veteran
vibrant
vice

victory
view
vigil
virgin
virtue
virtuous
visceral
visible
vista
vital
vitamin
vivacious
vivid
voluminous

W
waltz
warm
warmhearted
wash
wasted
wasteful
water
wave
wavy
weak
weakling
wealthy
weapon
wedded
weird
welcome
well-bred
well-known
western
whale
whirl
whistle

white-collar
white-hot
wholesome
widespread
wilt
window
windproof
windswept
windy
wintry
wise
wistful
witch
witty
wolfish
wonderful
worldly
worldwide

X
xenophobic

Y
yes-man
young
youthful

Z
zany
zeal
zest
zesty
zombie
zoned
zoo

Words and
Pictures

In any form of classified advertising, including traditional personal ads, line space is at a premium. That's why, in the print medium, common abbreviations for frequently included information have evolved. Traditionally, many of these abbreviations are grouped together with marital status—or sexual orientation for gay and bisexual people—listed first, race listed second, and sex listed third. Occasionally, the list contains four abbreviations; in those cases, religion is listed second—with racial identity third, and sex fourth. Examples of combinations include:

SWF for single white female
GWM for gay white male
SCWM for single Christian white male

Other abbreviations, such as ISO (in search of), go in the middle of a sentence or, like D/DF (drug- and disease-free), go at the end of the ad.

Common Abbreviations

A	Asian	**ISO**	In search of
B	Black or Buddhist	**J**	Jewish
BI	Bisexual	**L**	Latin
C	Christian	**LTR**	Long-term relationship
D	Divorced	**M**	Male or married
D/DF	Drug- and disease-free	**P**	Protestant
F	Female	**S**	Single
G	Gay	**W**	White or widowed
H	Hispanic		

A set of common, recognizable symbols, referred to by most as emoticons, has evolved in the electronic medium. Emoticons are sometimes called "smileys," because they resemble the little smiley faces that some people put in their handwritten letters. Emoticons help clarify intentions and add texture to a person's copy. To decipher them, just turn your head sideways and the symbols should form little pictures. If you're targeting computer-literate people, there's no reason you can't use these symbols in other media.

Common Emoticons

To find variations on the following emoticons as well as a more comprehensive list, see *Love Bytes* by David Fox (published by The Waite Group in 1995).

:-<	Broken Heart	:-D	Laugh
:/	Chagrin	:[	Pout
:'(	Cry	--<--<---@	A rose
:-)..	Drool	:-O	Scream
<:-)	Dunce	:C	Shocked
:(	Frown	:)	Smile
:->	Happy	:p	Stick out tongue
{}	Hug	;)	Wink
:*	Kiss	:O	Yell

Overview of *Media Options*

	Easy	Tried & True	Cutting Edge	Fast	Publicity Generating	Highly Targeted	Inexpensive	Less Competitive	Discreet
Newspaper Classified Ad	✔	✔					✔		✔
Magazine Classified Ad	✔					✔			✔
Newspaper Display Ad			✔					✔	
Magazine Display Ad			✔			✔		✔	
Outdoor Billboard			✔		✔			✔	
Community Bulletin Board	✔			✔		✔	✔		
Television			✔						
Radio			✔						✔
Internet & Online Chat				✔	✔				
Internet & Online Bulletin Board				✔	✔				

Whatever your goal, there is a media option right for you.

Response
Log

Photocopy this page and use one sheet for each response. Be sure to fill in as much information as possible and save these sheets for your records in case you run your ad again.

Ad Info

My Ad: _____

_____

_____

_____

Publication or medium & location:

_____

Date(s) the ad ran: _____ Costs involved: _____

Respondent Profile

Respondent's Name: _____

Date of response: _____

Address: _____

Home phone: _____

Employer: _____

Work phone: _____

Age: _____

Marital status: _____ Any children: _____

Key facts:

_____

_____

_____

Relevant health issues:

_____

Contact Info

Date contacted: _____

Quick reference (Circle one.):   Yes!   No   ?

Impressions:

_____

_____

Meeting Info

Day/date/time: _____

Place: _____

Outcome:

_____

_____

Appendix E

Suggested Reading *and* *Bibliographic Notes*

Advertising Copywriting

Bendinger, Bruce, *The Copy Workshop Workbook,* Chicago: The Copy Workshop, 1993.

Bly, Robert W., *The Copywriter's Handbook: Updated Editions,* New York: Henry Holt and Company, 1990.

Herzbrun, David, *Copywriting by Design,* Lincolnwood, IL: NTC Business Books, 1997.

Minsky, Laurence, and Emily Thornton Calvo, *How to Succeed in Advertising When All You Have Is Talent,* Lincolnwood, IL: NTC Business Books, 1994.

Reeves, Rosser, *Reality in Advertising,* New York: Alfred A. Knopf, 1961.

Dating

DeAngelis, Barbara, *The Real Rules: How to Find the Right Man for the Real You,* New York: Dell Publishing, 1997.

Fielding, William J., *Strange Customs of Courtship and Marriage,* New York: Hart Publishing, 1942.

Fox, David, *Love Bytes: The On-Line Dating Handbook,* Madera, CA: The Waite Group, 1995.

Haynes, Cyndi, and Dale Edwards, *2002 Things to Do on a Date,* Holbrook, MA: Bob Adams, Inc. Publishers, 1992.

Kelton, Nancy Davidoff, *Dating Is About Finding Someone So You Never Have to Date Again,* Kansas City, KS: Andrew and McMeel, 1995.

Kuriansky, Dr. Judy, *The Complete Idiot's Guide to Dating*, New York: Alpha Books, 1996.

Lowndes, Leil, *How to Make Anyone Fall in Love with You*, Lincolnwood, IL: NTC/Contemporary Publishing Group, 1995.

McWilliams, Peter, *Love 101: To Love Oneself Is the Beginning of a Lifelong Romance*, Santa Monica, CA: Prelude Press, 1995.

Neville, Lee, "Heart Trouble," *U.S. News & World Report*, V122, N5, February 10, 1997, page 16.

Sills, Judith, Ph.D., *How to Stop Looking for Someone Perfect and Find Someone to Love*, New York: Ballantine Books, 1989.

Stehling, Wendy, *How to Find a Husband in 30 Days*, New York: Pinnacle Books, 1985.

Warren, Neil Clark, Ph.D., *Finding the Love of Your Life*, New York: Pocket Books, 1992.

Personal-Ad Writing

Hinckley, Kathy, and Peter Hesse, *Plain Fat Chick Seeks Guy Who Likes Broccoli*, Salt Lake City: A Peregrine Smith Book, 1997.

Stein, M. L., "Expanding Your Personal Ads," *Editor and Publisher*, V13, N9, March 1, 1997, page 20.

Treen, Joe, "Lethal White Female," *People*, V38, N10, September 7, 1992, page 65.

Personal Safety

Bittenbinder, J. J., and Neal William, *Tough Target: A Street-Smart Guide to Staying Safe*, Philadelphia: Running Press, 1997.

De Becker, Gavin, *The Gift of Fear*, Boston: Little, Brown and Company, 1997.

Relationships and Self Help

Baber, Asa, *Naked at Gender Gap: A Man's View of the War Between the Sexes*, New York: Birch Lane Press, 1992.

Burns, David, M.D., *Intimate Connections*, New York: William Morrow and Co., Inc. 1985.

DeAngelis, Barbara, *Are You the One for Me?* New York: Island Books, 1992.

Gray, John, *Men Are from Mars: Women Are from Venus*, New York: HarperCollins, 1992.

Haynes, Cyndi, and Dale Edwards, *2002 Ways to Attract and Keep a Mate,* Holbrook, MA: Bob Adams, Inc. Publishers, 1996.

James, Larry, *Love Notes for Lovers,* Scottsdale, AZ: Career Assurance Press, 1995.

Jeffers, Susan, *Feel the Fear and Do It Anyway,* New York: Fawcett Books, 1992.

Luchetti, Cathy, *I Do!: Courtship, Love, and Marriage on the American Frontier,* New York: Crown Trade Paperback, 1996.

Page, Susan, *If I'm So Wonderful, Why Am I Still Single?* New York: Viking Penguin, Inc., 1988.

Popcorn, Faith, *The Popcorn Report,* New York: Doubleday, 1991.

———, and Lys Marigold, *Clicking: 16 Trends to Future Fit Your Life, Your Work, and Your Business,* New York: HarperCollins, 1996.

Schlessinger, Laura, Ph.D. *How Could You Do That? The Abdication of Character, Courage, and Conscience,* New York: HarperCollins, 1996.

Sills, Judith, *Excess Baggage,* New York: Penguin Books, 1993.

———, *How to Stop Looking for Someone Perfect and Find Someone to Love,* New York: Ballantine Books, 1989.